Now Network

NOW NETWORK

Helping professionals enjoy the unavoidable

Adrian Priddle

Girder & Joist Editions
Cambridge

Published by Girder & Joist Editions
(an imprint of Off the Page Ideas Limited, Cambridge, England)

The moral rights of the author have been asserted.

Development Editor
Sheila Bounford

ISBN 978-0-9933686-0-8 (print)
ISBN 978-0-9933686-1-5 (kindle)

CONTENTS

ACKNOWLEDGEMENTS

I would like to acknowledge the help of many people who contributed to the writing of this book, most importantly those who have supported my career and provided moments of impactful direction. I will always be thankful for these, and I must particularly thank Stuart Woodward at Deloitte and Stewart Beamont for their guidance at key moments.

My good friends and colleagues have read and provided feedback, and I thank Anne Jones, Kaye Bateman, Jonathan Geard-Beney, Andy Norton and Stewart Beamont for their suggestions and honest advice.

Finally, thanks are due to all my clients and colleagues who have helped me throughout my career which, in the end, is a collection of experiences made all the more valuable by the people I shared them with.

PART 1

Networking Matters

MY
NETWORKING
LIFE

How networking helped me

Networking is key to all professionals developing their business, their capabilities and their careers. It has been essential throughout my career. Successful networking helped me to progress in a professional service firm, allowed me to meet many interesting people whose company I have enjoyed and whose knowledge I have benefited from, and has enabled me to build a consulting business with a wide range of clients.

Looking back on the networking I did in the early years of my career as an auditor at Deloitte, it was nearly all entirely accidental, arising as it did out of the work situations I was placed in. I was an unconscious networker, getting to know new contacts through the work I was assigned to do. In retrospect I can see that my interest in others, my passion for learning more about them, for understanding what made them tick and whether I could help, was key to making and taking opportunities.

After a while, it gradually became clear that merely providing a technical service or excellence would only take me so far, which is a realisation that eventually dawns on most professionals in some form of service industry. I needed to build a network, build a specialism and become known for something. This is when I first had to ask myself the question, "How do I do this without feeling like a salesman - I'm an accountant". The need to be *authentically me* had begun to raise its head, fighting against my perception that to succeed in networking I needed to be something very different from what I was.

I chose to network in a way that suited my strengths and so began to develop a thought-through strategy for my networking. I used my love of football to create events that involved a lunchtime gathering before heading out for a game. I organised these through client contacts involved in football and through the internal contacts I had made with fellow professionals at Deloitte. In so doing I created events that people enjoyed and looked forward to, whilst building deeper relationships with potential new clients and sharing the opportunity with colleagues in the office.

The range of other networking opportunities in a 'Big Four' firm also provided plenty of business and social gatherings for developing relationships and meeting new people. I picked those where I felt new contacts would be interested in hearing about the service I provided, or I felt I could add value by attending. Value did not mean I knew anything special, it may be that I just introduced people to each other. This approach meant that for a long time the events I attended remained in my comfort zone.

It was only much later that I realised how lucky I had been to have so many opportunities on hand.

What I discovered about networking was the more I did, the more it paid back to me. The more people I connected with, the wider the networks I could link into. The more networks I was linked into, the greater the number of possibilities created. The more possibilities, the easier it became to gain introductions to people or to arrange to meet people I wanted to see.

The more I networked (it seemed to me), the luckier I became in meeting helpful or interesting people. Of course I wasn't lucky at all: I was putting myself in those situations, substantially increasing my chances of meeting the right people. I was introducing myself more often and so the points I made and the questions I drew out became more targeted and helpful to others. I became more practised in handling a range of business and social topics and I found my brain and attention outside work began to take on board subjects from the TV, radio and newspapers that might make interesting conversation. The desire to network, and getting better at networking, expanded my world view and made me a more rounded, better informed individual.

If, when I left Client Service in Deloitte and moved into a role managing aspects of their Learning and Development offering, I initially thought that all that external networking might lose its value to me, I could not have been more wrong. I still needed my external contact network: it provided me with valuable insight into the marketplace. Instead of looking for business opportunities for my employer, I was now listening to ensure the learning content I was sourcing was up-to-date and relevant.

I was now supporting professionals in Deloitte, and I had very demanding clients: the partners, directors, managers and staff who used our learning services. These stakeholders became my new client network and I helped ensure the quality of what we delivered for them through maintaining my engagement with my external network. One of the beauties of networking is that once you have met people and added them to your network, you can maintain the contact and stay in touch, meaning you don't lose them. How you work with your network and how they work with you will change throughout your career, but if you are part of each other's network you will always have the opportunity to be helpful.

At the same time I needed to improve my internal network: I needed breadth and depth, from trainees to the executive partner board. A mix of the very informal (coffees, chats in the cafeteria, opportunities taken in reception or near elevators and in the places where people gathered) and the very formal (presentations to board level, budget reviews and debriefings from committees) enabled me to do this. Informal chats are easy to undervalue, but they can be priceless. At Deloitte this kind of conversation helped me to understand more about the people I was providing services to. Conversations without an agenda can be very valuable in exploring what people are feeling and thinking.

Eventually my time at Deloitte ended and, as with many people mid-career, this led me to the challenge of building my own business, and utilising the networks I had in order to create new value, new ideas and fresh opportunities. I had already been lucky to have a great career with a great employer, and thereafter Deloitte became a great client.

However one client does not make for a sustainable business. I needed to grow my network to a level at which it would provide more revenue sources and more opportunities. For anyone moving into business, either as a small venture or as a self-employed individual, those early days when you wonder, "Will people want to buy what I offer?" are pretty scary. But for me, the time I had invested in my network of client contacts, fellow professionals, and suppliers of learning and consulting services proved invaluable. My network was a support to give me encouragement, to listen to my concerns, offer advice and, where possible, helpful action. It was a network that provided my initial contracts of work, either as an individual or as part of a team.

My business was all about the choice, design and delivery of learning and development programmes. Obviously I had some immediate advantages in certain sectors: being an accountant and auditor was helpful in the professional and corporate environment. Moreover, I had been able to experiment with my views on learning and development whilst at Deloitte, so I went into the market with energy and ideas. Building on my experience, I initially focused on business development and management skills. Over time, this has developed into a closer focus on business development, commercial awareness and leadership development.

To succeed in my business, I needed new contacts that

could either introduce me to the type of work I could add value to (for example other consultancies where I could align myself or have an associate arrangement) or to direct buyers. Again, I prioritised the external network of potential new clients I wanted to create. To reach them I invested time in attending events at relevant membership organisations; going to seminars I was invited to by professional service firms; and signing up for local business groups and offerings.

I found myself relearning some of the old lessons about how to network, but also found myself in the fast growing world of social media. Leaving Deloitte in 2003 coincided with the beginning of my experience of Facebook and LinkedIn. The impact of LinkedIn for me has been threefold:

- Finding and exchanging ideas with individuals I would never previously have had the chance to connect with.
- Following up with people who I have met at an event or a training course has become much easier with LinkedIn as a resource to facilitate reconnecting with people after events.
- Building a profile for the work I do for a wider audience, enabling discussion and knowledge sharing with others in the sectors I work in.

In building my business, I have stretched my networking skills and moved way beyond my earlier comfort zone. The most uncomfortable, but nevertheless the most rewarding experiences for me are exhibitions and conferences, which by their very nature and format offer multiple opportunities for short conversations. Creating a favourable, memorable impact in such a short period of time is a real challenge. In this high-pressure, rapid-fire environment I discovered the clearest proof of the value of what I have come to call *authentic networking*.

At exhibitions and conferences I discovered that just relaxing and being myself, rather than trying to schmooze or coax people into conversations, proved the most successful approach. There are two reasons why this works best. Firstly, when we relax and don't put on an act, it feels real to both parties: no games being played, no careful management of the conversation, just an engaging chat about whatever is of interest. Secondly, this authentic approach gives the other person an immediate insight into who I am and how I work. I am able to give people a glimpse of what working with me might feel like, the types of conversation we will have, and the potential ways I might be able to help them achieve their goals. I am not saying I am 100% successful, but somewhat counter-intuitively, just relaxing is a powerful approach and creates genuine connections.

By attending exhibitions and conferences, I also discovered at these events that there was a whole host of sectors I hadn't experienced. My career at Deloitte had taken me into retail, football and manufacturing. Now I was building contacts in financial services, health and safety, precision engineering and housing associations – to name but a few. Once again, networking was widening my experience, building my knowledge, and presenting me with new challenges; I enjoyed learning what made people passionate about these businesses, the challenges they faced and working out how and where I could possibly help.

Of course, networking snowballs: by making new contacts at new organisations, I was then also introduced to their contacts in those organisations. I gradually became more proactive about asking for referrals to others, or for introductions to key stakeholders. This was facilitated by the fact that my initial contacts had a very good picture of who I was and what I had to offer. As a result of my being authentic and open in our initial contacts, my contacts were confident to vouch for me when introducing me to their colleagues.

I have become more and more convinced that we are at our best networking when we put aside any thought of 'selling' and show people more of ourselves, whether that be bold and extrovert or reflective and considered. The good thing is that different personalities appeal to different people. Relationships built on authenticity from the outset have the potential to last not just for a few months or until after the first piece of work you do together is finished: they become part of your network, built throughout your career and through which you can provide value and help to each other in the long term.

This book gives you a range of tips based on what works for me, and what I have successfully coached others to do over the years. Take the tips that work for you and, more importantly, the ones that feel like you can really deliver as part of your approach. This way you can be the best authentic networker you can and enjoy the benefits of long-lasting business relationships.

HOW THIS
BOOK WORKS

Structure

I have split this book into three parts, plus a conclusion of course.

You are reading **Part 1** now. It is a general introduction to networking: why it matters, why it is difficult and what we can do about it. I give a brief overview of my own experience of networking and how it has improved and developed over the years.

Part 2 sets the scene for *your* networking, looks at preparing to network and the activities and additional approaches you can take to get more out of your networking. Part 2 looks at:
- Networking attitude
- Networking strategy
- Personal impact
- Preparation.

To ensure you give your best to your networking and therefore get the best results and return, both in the short and the long term, it is important to consider all four of these. To use a construction industry metaphor, these provide the groundwork and the foundations for building strong networks.

Part 3 covers the four stages of GLAD Networking:

- **Greeting**: meeting new people and forming an initial impression with them.
- **Learning**: building your understanding of your new contacts, their interests and their businesses.
- **Attracting**: creating the links that allow you to continue building the relationship later, demonstrating to your contacts that it is worth staying in touch.
- **Developing**: building relationships through how you maintain contact and what you offer within a potential new relationship.

Each chapter contains tips, prompts and ideas

If you don't have much time or need some quick impetus, then the structure of this book should facilitate dipping in and out. Each chapter starts with some context setting, overview points and exploration of what we are talking about. After that you will find a series of tips on specific areas of activity to help you. These tips provide some explanation, experiences and examples from my networking and training, and then finish with a box of prompts and ideas. If you want to go straight to some points to jolt your thinking or to give you a new idea, then these boxes will help.

Some of the tips will overlap between chapters. For example, there are tips that are part of the section on *Preparation* that could also apply to *Networking Strat-*

egy. Also, many tips on learning more about our contacts and building great conversations in *Personal Impact* and *Developing* overlap with each other. This is in the nature of networking: all the tasks involved are interconnected.

What networking are we talking about?

The answer to this is simple: *any conversation*. It doesn't matter whether you are at work, in a meeting with a client or colleagues, at a seminar, conference, organized event or online. All these are just the different environments in which we network, try to build relationships, meet new people and ultimately achieve our objectives, be they professional or personal. It is fashionable to disaggregate subjects (into short blog posts for content marketing, for example), as this can create a greater volume of books, training inputs and specialisms. However, successful GLAD Networking is about authenticity, and by definition requires lateral thinking and an ability to segue between subjects and categories.

Today's business world incorporates technology into almost everything we do, so it seems strange to separate it out when considering networking. This book addresses networking as practice and behaviour, and considers the differences in environment (physical or digital) only where such differences directly impact interactions. When I talk about being proactive, that doesn't mean just going to lots of events, it is about how you approach everything in networking including preparation for events, meeting new clients, managing your online profiles and engaging in research. If you are developing your networking strategy or plan, it needs to consider how you will leverage your existing network and customers, how you will use internal and external sources of networking and which social media platforms best suit your aims.

At its simplest, networking in my terms is about aiming to build new relationships, which happens in a variety of situations and environments. The skills you need lie in the conversations and interactions you have with others and the strategies we develop to facilitate them, whether those conversations are in person or online, by phone or by email. My focus in this book is on building those skills and strategies.

What gets in the way?

We all seem to know the theory. Most of us have been on courses or had appraisals that have emphasised the importance of networking to us. We have seen other people be successful at networking and wondered how they do it. So what is it that gets in the way and why do we have such an ability to identify, or imagine, barriers when faced with the need for action?

During my experience of facilitating networking workshops and coaching professionals I have heard a range of reasons why people can't or won't network and all of these reasons can be summarised in one of the following categories:

Task versus relationship

Many barriers are, in essence, about the fact that people

prefer to *achieve a task* rather than *invest in a relationship*. Whether that is because the task is more urgent or important to them or because it is easier for them to control and measure, this barrier is about not placing enough value on the building of new relationships.

Context

Many professionals believe that what they do is so specialist that networking does not apply to them. Either they develop business purely from the excellence of what they do, or people aren't involved or interested in their business. I would argue that even if you are excellent at what you do you need to network so that more contacts and customers can discover your excellence. If you believe your business doesn't involve people making decisions, then take another look: you've probably missed something (are you really talking to machines all day long?).

Genuine or fake

One of the most universal barriers I hear is that networking makes people 'feel fake'. When networking these people often try to take on new personalities in the belief this is what is expected when networking and therefore find the experience extremely uncomfortable. This is easy to cure: stop being fake and be who you are. You may not win every bit of business going, but you are more likely to win business and develop recurring customers.

Time

Really? "I don't have the time," or, "I'm too busy!" are the oldest excuses in the book for almost anything we feel uncomfortable doing. It is called procrastination, and all but the most self-disciplined of us do it. The reality is often that we *are* busy, but rarely are we *too* busy. The truth is more often that we don't want to face our discomfort or that we don't rate networking as important enough in our priority list to be worthy of our time. Even when we know investing time now will save time later (short- *v.* long-term benefits) we will still say it is too difficult to find the time. Networking in this respect is a close relation of that other long-term management skill: delegation.

Objective (aim)

If we don't acknowledge an aim, a point or a goal for our networking it is very easy to find reasons not to do it. After all, most other tasks or demands on our time have a very clear purpose. We may need to produce some output for our boss, or reply to a client: the aim of the task is clear, and that clarity pushes it further up our priority list. The phrase "What is the point?" is a real, pointed question: "What *is* the point of *your* networking?" Ask yourself; because if you don't know what the point is, then why haven't you tried to answer that question?

Fear

Fear is probably at the root of most other objections: the simple and straightforward fear of meeting somebody new; the risk we perceive that they won't like us, or that we won't have anything helpful to say; or worse still that we will say something stupid, or somehow show ourselves up. All of these are fears that can arise, but as networking is not a popularity contest, or about appearing to be the cleverest or the most entertaining in the room, the majority of such fears are unfounded. We can also take steps ahead of networking (*see* Part 1) that will prepare us for networking, build our confidence in what we are doing, and in so doing tackle these fears.

Returns

The desire to achieve a quick return on efforts can easily become a barrier. We start networking and wonder why the new business and sales haven't come flooding in. But a return on investment often needs patience and willingness to build for the long term, rather than demanding an instant result and declaring the activity 'a waste of time'. Our expectations of return and our understanding of what we are trying to achieve need to be realistic. As with many events, it is better to have modest expectations and be pleasantly surprised, than have high expectations and be constantly disappointed.

It is all about you

Of course all the barriers listed above are just perspectives we use to rationalise a lack of networking, to excuse the discomfort it causes or, worst of all, to avoid the necessity to do it. If you approach networking with a more positive mindset, then you are less likely to waste your intellect and imagination identifying barriers. None of them is a real obstacle: the tips and the challenges in this book provide easy ways to overcome each and every barrier you can imagine.

It is key to remember that successful networking involves

remaining true to yourself, being genuine in your interactions with others and, therefore, creating an authentic impact on others. If, when you network, you behave like somebody else, your contacts will be deprived of the opportunity to learn your true value and what it feels like to work with you. If you adopt a false networking persona it will begin to feel like networking is fake, or a scenario that is acted out. So my tips are about how *you* prepare for networking by focusing on making the most of *your* strengths and give people the best impression of who *you* are. You, not a temporary version of you, are the business person your new contacts want to get to know.

When you first meet people it is natural to want to create a great first impression, but this needs to be sustainable. If you exaggerate your behaviour or overstate any claims, then it will become clear later and create a sense of disappointment. You are more likely to build long-lasting contacts and relationships if people get to meet the real you and gain a sense of what you can genuinely help them with. Even in the short term you can cause yourself difficulty by overselling yourself or demonstrating a confidence that is not matched by your examples, your stories, and your track record. It is always a mistake to over-sell and under-deliver.

Another aspect of focusing on you is about what you take from this book: look for what will work for you in your style and with your personality and strengths. I would love to claim every tip and point suitable for everyone, but they will not be. There is a range of ideas and tips from which you need to select techniques that work for you. Identify where you could improve your networking, where could you use some new ideas, or where you could try some new approaches. If something already works for you and fits with the way you do things then carry on with that approach.

Finally, if you do create a plan for your networking from this book and its tips - as I hope you will - please make it a *realistic* and *achievable* one. In fact if it isn't realistic and achievable, I will have failed in my purpose. If you set unrealistic goals you will only set yourself up to imagine a whole range of reasons and barriers not to carry on. Identify what you want to achieve, and then break your aim down into stages you can accommodate and achieve in your working days, and that you feel comfortable to commit to.

Be positive. Be you. Enjoy your networking!

WHAT IS GLAD NETWORKING?

GLAD Networking

GLAD is a simple acronym I use for the four-stage process that follows any successful contact, from the first meeting through to developing a working relationship. Helpfully, 'glad' is also a positive emotion: meeting new people and building new possibilities through relationships and business should be something we feel good about. It doesn't need to be the chore or the burden that many feel it is: an external requirement placed on them by a line manager or a boss who needs to improve revenue or profit performance. Yes, profit and revenue gains are positive outcomes of networking and may well be your goals, but they are not the whole picture and it should not feel like you have to change yourself in order to rise to the challenge.

The four stages of GLAD Networking are:
- Greet
- Learn
- Attract
- Develop.

Part 2 of this book covers each of these four stages in depth, but to begin with it is helpful to consider them as a whole because networking is not just a single conversation, but rather an ongoing activity from meeting a new contact through to building and sustaining a business relationship. Great networking leads to new relationships, and the maintenance and building of those relationships is a continuous process. It is all too easy to focus on the first three stages: *Greet, Learn* and *Attract,* which are often condensed into a short space of time as, for example, at an event, seminar or conference, but to neglect the fourth stage, *Develop,* until much later. To do so risks wasting all the hard work and working up of courage that it took you to start networking in the first place: people quickly forget once they are back to their daily work.

GLAD Networking should also help you to develop a positive impact on those you meet. Having a positive approach, using encouraging vocabulary and behaviours and valuing the interactions you have, as well as the knowledge you gain, will all contribute to a positive experience for the people you meet and develop relationships with. In turn, they will communicate this positive impression of you on to others.

The GLAD acronym is intended to help you to easily remember what makes for successful networking, and to be positive about the networking you do. If you aren't keen on the labels for the stages, just have a look at the ideas and actions in this book without worrying about the titles. As in many situations in life, the actions you take are more important than the labels you hang on them. So look into the activities and ideas offered and, if you prefer, rename them with labels, prompts and reminders that work or are more comfortable for you. Consider how you could improve your networking and enjoy it more, and if you find ways of doing so you will have gained what I intended from this book.

Successful networking, GLAD Networking, requires you to take the long view because it is about taking opportunities to meet new people and *then* building *sustainable* relationships with them. I don't mean by this that you need to read this book all at once: we all know most business books are rarely read to the end and almost never from front to back. If you are looking at a particular challenge in a part of the process then dip in and out to see what ideas you can take away. However, do not lose sight of the reality that whatever challenges you the most, whatever it is that has prompted you to pick up this book, networking is not about a single challenge or series of challenges. GLAD Networking is a virtuous circle that becomes easier, more successful and more enjoyable as you progress, and can become a rewarding continuum of your professional life.

PART 2

You and Your Networking

YOUR NETWORKING ATTITUDE

What is a networking attitude?

Your attitude towards networking, particularly in the first moments of making a contact, will be key to how you come across and the level of success you have in building and growing your network. It may sound obvious, but *you* are the person everyone in *your* network gets to meet. Over the course of time they will experience conversations, catch-ups and possibly even project work and business meetings with you. So is your attitude to meeting people and sustaining contact with them a good one? Are you proactive about it? Do you look forward to learning more about others? Do you prepare for meeting people and think about how to create a strong impression without being overpowering of overbearing?

For me, the best networking attitude can be described as a mindset that is alert to networking opportunities in all interactions and then makes the most of those opportunities by making interaction comfortable and easy for the other person. A networking attitude looks positively for what can be gained by meeting new people or building relationships with existing contacts - for both parties. The best of networking attitudes looks beyond the immediate work or tasks and seeks to build a network that will help create more work and tasks for the future. Although this attitude ultimately benefits the skilled networker, their key concerns whilst they are networking revolve around the other person and how they feel.

To check whether you have a good networking attitude, ask yourself some of the questions below, and be really honest about it.

- Do you think about your network on a frequent and regular basis?
- If so, how often?
- Have you thought out a networking strategy or plan to help you choose the right networking options to take?
- Before going to business meetings or running workshops do you consider what opportunities may arise for networking?
- When meeting someone new are you keen to learn more about them and to understand what they do at work or socially?
- Do you look at your diary and consider where a networking opportunity might present itself? For example, linking a business appointment with catching up with an existing or a potential contact.
- How do you split your thinking time between what you want to do and what they want?
- When you meet someone new, are you likely to make a follow-up contact within a couple of weeks?
- Do you consider how the other person would

prefer to keep up or communicate with you - face to face, telephone, online?

If you said *no* or *not really*, to many of these questions, then there is probably some work you can do to put yourself into a more positive space when networking and to respond to opportunities more proactively.

If you said *yes* to many of them, then you are already adopting a positive networking attitude, either intuitively or intentionally – which will make many of the ideas offered in this book easier for you to adopt and implement.

Where can you work on it?

Attitude is an internal state. It can be affected by many factors, both internal and external, including events in our working day, our personality, our preferences, other people's choices, and the ups and downs we all experience. But although attitude is an internal state, we can make choices about how to manage ourselves that can have a high impact on our attitude and even shift us from a negative or neutral state to a positive one.

Your networking attitude can be built up or undermined by the messages you allow your 'inner voices' to give. It is all too easy to indulge in a diet of, "I'm too busy to network," or even worse, "Why would they want to talk to me?" So you need to actively choose from a different menu of *positive* reasons to network, *clarity* about your strategy, *reminders* of what other people want from good business or social relationships, and build your confidence when interacting with others.

The action you need to take to work on your networking attitude will depend upon your character and your preferences, which will have created your personal 'attitude barrier'. You may find it easy to talk with people at conferences, but somehow never manage to follow up when you are back in the office. Or conversely you may find conversation excruciating, but be very diligent about following up when you have talked to someone new. Whatever your attitude barrier, you need to create a positive framework around the whole of the networking experience, and a level of comfort or confidence that helps you to be proactive in all its stages. This may involve:

- Creating a strategy or plan for your networking.
- Increasing the level of contact focus in your preparation by, for example, considering your networking from your contacts' points of view and not your own.
- Improving your attitude to following up with new contacts.
- Developing a range of ways of approaching people, for example face to face as well as online.
- Recognising where you have strengths for networking and relationships, as well as where you can develop further.

Networking is present and part of your work every day. Most of us meet new people and add to our network of relationships through the work we do, and if you are reading this book, it is likely that this is the case for you too. Therefore, developing a positive attitude to networking allows you to maximise all the opportunities that accrue during your normal business day. Thinking about networking as something that pervades your everyday work may even reduce your need for more deliberate 'out of your comfort zone' networking events. It can also have a positive impact on your overall wellbeing, because a positive attitude reduces stress and anxiety.

Later in the book there are particular tips based around strategy, preparation, developing contacts and regular consideration of the merits of face-to-face and online networking. Meanwhile, the tips below will help you to think about your networking attitude and where you could improve its positivity and therefore its impact upon your networking success.

Tip 1: Networking is just having conversations

But conversations only happen if you want them to, wherever you want to have them

It is easy to over complicate networking, yet it is only about having conversations, so networking is something we do consciously or subconsciously every day. People who are great networkers don't even think of it as networking: they are merely having conversations with people they know or people they would like to know.

The reality is that all of us are networking whenever we talk to each other. In conversation with a client or with a customer you have known for a long time you are still exchanging information, showing an interest in each other and, hopefully, looking to help each other out. This is high-quality networking. Depending on personal preferences, work culture and industry practice you may prefer the face-to-face conversation to online networking and social media – but ultimately it is all conversation.

Technology provides new ways to have conversations with each other, learn about each other and discuss opinions. Even where interaction is online, we are still participating in conversations and we are therefore still networking. Technology makes our networks closer and yet broader, bringing us frequent, bite-sized chunks of information and constant updates on peoples' new qualifications and changes in job roles and responsibilities. These online conversations mean we also know far more about what interests our contacts through their blog posts, articles and updates, all neatly digested, depending on how we configure our settings.

A successful networking plan will create conversations and will have considered how to utilise both face-to-face networking and online opportunities. It will include and make use of a number of factors:

- Your networking goal in terms of the size of network you are aiming for, the types of interaction you seek, and the way you prefer to utilise your network.
- Your personal preferences: to come across in an authentic manner and not to feel fake or insincere in your approach.
- Finding networking opportunities that meet your goals: there is no point networking where your target contacts are not active.

Great conversations can happen face-to-face *and* online, so don't limit yourself to one environment: focus on having great conversations wherever they are. Great conversations are the start of great relationships.

Prompts and ideas

- Look at your diary at the start of the day. Identify the networking opportunities. Where can you start a new relationship? Where will you build on existing ones? Identify anything you can do to maximise opportunities.
- Focus on the quality of the conversation. A great conversation can be had online by email, in a forum or on Twitter just as easily as face to face.
- Think about how your face-to-face activities and your online networking are meeting the goals of your networking strategy. The balance of activity should be part of your strategy and the actions you take should link back to this.

Tip 2: Networking is a relationship business

So invest in relationships over time and the returns will come

'Networking' is a generic word we use for all the activities that begin and develop our relationships, be they personal or professional. Networking activities can take many forms but their objectives are either to find new people or to make the opportunity to get to know existing contacts better. These activities happen in a wide variety of contexts: work, social events, online; and also for a wide variety of reasons including business development, profile building, learning and career planning. The timeframe over which networking delivers results can vary significantly, from days to years.

In his book *The 7 Habits of Highly Effective People,* [1] Stephen R. Covey describes the idea of the emotional bank account, saying that if we have sufficient deposits in our relationships with others then we will have the opportunity to make occasional withdrawals should we need to. Networking is the start of these accounts and our ability to build relationships will depend upon our willingness to make deposits, such as:

- Staying in touch over the long term, not just being there when there is income to be made and disappearing when there isn't.
- Providing useful introductions to others in our network when they are helpful.
- Giving helpful information and advice, without always attaching a bill to it.

Just every so often you will get really lucky. You will be standing with someone at the right event or sat next to someone at a conference or meeting and they will be someone who needs your help and services at that moment in time, and whilst that is a form of luck, you have made your own luck by being there. Clearly the more you network, the greater the chances you will be next to the right person at the right time. In this sense you do indeed make your own luck.

But having struck lucky, or made your luck, it is essential to remember that Rome was not built in a day. Networking is a long game, not a quick win. Taking the long view will bring returns to you when people remember who has been with them along their particular journey. Over a period of time a contact is able to build a strong understanding of your skills and expertise, and finally they trust you enough to know that you will deliver in the way they want.

Trusted relationships built for the long haul may not bring quick returns, but once built, both parties enjoy the benefits time and time again.

Prompts and ideas

- Networking is the activity that helps us to build new relationships: it's not about immediate selling but about starting a relationship where either business or personal achievements can be sought.
- Invest in your emotional bank accounts for people in your network: be ready to make a deposit in building the relationship as you never know when you may need to make a withdrawl.
- The long-term approach builds trust that will last in a business relationship, meaning that when the opportunity does come, it isn't a one off.

Tip 3: Networking is only fake when you make it fake

Be you, be real, be interested and then it is genuine

One of the greatest challenges many people have with networking is the belief that to be a great networker they need to be someone different, more 'interesting' or 'exciting'. This fear manifests itself in a range of ways that conspire to leave us feeling that what we are doing is fake.

The best advice is to be you, and to trust that others are also being themselves. As with internet dating, it is a very bad idea to pretend to be something other than you really are. When networking, you stand the best chance of success if the real you is the person any new contacts meet. If you present a persona that is different from the real you, then people may be disappointed later on when you turn out to be different. That's if you get that far. More likely, the act of trying to be something different will come across as insincere and will be a turn-off from the very beginning.

What do you need to do to be more genuine and authentic in your networking?
- Let go of any preconceptions about what makes a good networker: you are not aiming at perfection - you are trying to build new contacts and relationships for the real you.
- Calm and resist the inner voice that prompts you to try to be more entertaining, vocal, energetic or

noticeable, particularly if that behaviour is not naturally you.

- Be honest: so for example if you're not into a sport or a hobby the other person is, don't be afraid to acknowledge you've never been involved with it before; what *is* important is showing an interest in why *they* like it.
- Offer information about yourself: so if someone is talking football but you prefer horse riding, then engage in the discussion about which teams they are interested in, but be honest that you don't follow football but you do enjoy, for example, horse riding.
- Remember your goal is to *begin* building relationships. If they are to be successful then those relationships need strong foundations, not the shaky ones of a few fake facts made up in order to make you sound interesting. It is also highly unlikely that you will be offered a great business opportunity simply because you were an entertaining person to meet at a networking event.

As Oscar Wilde put it, "Be yourself. Everyone else is already taken."

Prompts and ideas

- Let people meet you, not some version of you that you believe they will want to do business with more. People can spot a fake and rarely enjoy doing business with them.
- Be prepared to be honest about your interests or involvements, but remain keen to learn about others.
- Not every great networker is an extrovert. You don't have to be entertaining, witty and talkative. For many people this is annoying and comes across as arrogant or showing off.
- The best business relationships are built on personal integrity, not on entertainment value.

Tip 4: People at events want to meet others

So help them by talking to them

Have you ever wondered what another person is thinking about you? Has this ever stopped you starting a conversation? It is all too easy to allow yourself to believe you have already been judged as boring, not worth talking to or overly sales-orientated. But turn this on its head and try putting yourself in the other person's shoes. Think about why *they* are there - most likely exactly the same reason that *you* are there.

Let's start with an invite to an event, seminar or conference. The organiser, host and sponsors all have reasons for staging the event, one of which is providing opportunities for networking and information exchange. You could opt out by refusing the invitation and asking to be sent the relevant information rather than attending. But if enough people do that, everyone loses out.

Even if you accept the initial invitation, there are options available to limit your networking on the day. You could not turn up, or arrive just in time; only go to any presentations you think will be interesting; answer email during breaks; and leave before the closing networking. I have been to many seminars where some delegates have arrived at the last moment, watched the presentations and left immediately. And yes, at times I have been one of those annoying people who said they would be there, then failed to show up. Everyone present, except the speakers and the organisers, had the same set of choices about whether to attend, and the spirit in which to attend. So if you find yourself face to face with some-one, then it is a fair bet they are willing to network and talk. They have had plenty of chances to refuse the invitation, or to absent themselves, and they haven't. So take the chance and be friendly.

Another good example of a situation where you can be confident in opening conversations, is a workshop or event with an existing client. The reason why you are invited is work-related, perhaps delivery of a project, or working on an opportunity or challenge they have. So straight away you have a point of common interest: you are working on the same problem; you have relevance to them; and they may well have information you will find interesting or even useful in your work. Workshops in particular are great places to avoid the evaluative thought process that tells you the opinions others 'will' have. You have been invited because you are important and relevant. Don't let that inner voice tell you otherwise.

Prompts and ideas

- Think about the situation from the other person's point of view. They too have a reason why they attended.
- So how about asking them what it was and seeing if you can help them meet their objective?
- Let go of your own assumptions - you are adding value by being present and communicative.
- Remind yourself of your value before you attend and when you are attending and take confidence from that value.
- There are few people who go to networking events and want to be left alone. Those people either didn't go or went home quickly. So talk to the people you meet and be friendly.
- You create a better impression by engaging with people than by ignoring them.

Tip 5: A work meeting offers networking opportunities

You just need to see who is there and want to talk with them

Networking is about your attitude as well as your skills. We have already seen that all conversations are networking opportunities. This tip is about encouraging you to look at your everyday meetings and work, which you may never have thought of as 'networking', and make better use of the opportunities presented by the ordinary and the 'everyday'.

Any meeting you have, by definition, involves other people, or it wouldn't be a 'meeting'. Meetings may involve colleagues, contacts, clients, supporters, influencers, decision-makers - whatever labels you choose to give them. If you look at them in the right way, you will see the new people we could meet, or further progress you could make with people you already know. Of course you have an immediate task or an objective to be achieved in the meeting, *but that is not all that's going on*. In achieving an objective you have the opportunity to build or damage relationships depending upon how you achieve it; so take a bit of time to consider the networking you could do (remember Stephen Covey's 'Emotional Bank Account' *see page 32*).

Making contact with someone via a work meeting provides you with a certain amount of access to *their* network, and the possibility of being introduced or even referred to others. When someone has seen you in operation at work, they feel more comfortable putting forward their opinion of you to others: they have first-hand experience and examples to offer. This makes 'at work' networking both a strong platform to work from, and important to get right.

Ask yourself some simple questions ahead of your next 'ordinary' business meeting or discussion, to help you shift from a 'business as usual' mindset to a 'proactive networking' mindset:

- Who will be at this meeting?
- Who do I know and who can I meet for the first time?
- What will they be looking for from me?
- How will they want me to deliver that?
- Who else will they know who I would like to meet or make contact with?

It is all about having that positive networking attitude - an attitude that sees all meetings and conversations at work as having more potential than just achieving the obvious. They are opportunities to meet, share, learn and connect. In short, to network.

Prompts and ideas

- Look for more from a meeting than just actions: build connections and relationships.
- In your meeting preparation ask yourself some networking-related questions to understand the possibilities this meeting might offer.
- Be courageous in asking others to introduce or refer you to the people they know.

Tip 6: Grasp opportunities to network

The one certainty of *not* networking is the list of things you will miss out on

This tip is the networking equivalent of 'seize the day'. Not networking means you will miss out on:

- Potential new relationships
- Potential new business
- New knowledge and ideas
- Industry perspectives
- Interesting discussions.

You will always be able to find reasons not to do something particularly when you are busy. You - like the rest of us - will need to push yourself to grasp the moment and go and have that conversation, or attend that seminar. Here are five really strong reasons why you should:

- You need new customers and clients to keep your career and businesses going. You may feel successful at retaining clients and customers right at this moment, but over time losing some is inevitable for reasons beyond your control. You are not immune from the need to top up your pipeline of business. If you network, you have a source of relationships and opportunities to do this.
- The outside world and new contacts provide fresh perspectives on what you do. These grow your expertise and knowledge as a professional or service provider, and enhance your value to your existing clients and contacts.
- Networking contributes to building your reputation.

Yes, delivering an excellent product or service is the foundation of a great reputation, but your networking provides opportunities to reach people who currently have no access to you. And often when you network, you are providing opportunities for existing contacts to speak positively about you.

- Returning to the piece of work you were doing with a fresh mind after you have been networking is likely to produce a fresh energy for it, and possibly some new ideas and thoughts: a change is as good as a rest.
- Taking networking opportunities provides variety and adds interest to your day, lifting your energy, well-being and sense of satisfaction in what you are doing.

Spend a couple of minutes thinking of your positive reasons to network: thinking about it will quell the natural predisposition to find reasons not to do it. With positive thoughts in mind, you will be able to make more balanced decisions on how to prioritise your time.

Prompts and ideas

- Ask yourself, "Is the task I am prioritising over my networking really *so* urgent and important that I will sacrifice future business or personal growth for it?" Sometimes the answer *will* be yes, but not as often as you may be inclined to default to.
- Look for the reasons why you should be networking rather than the excuses not to. There will always be something you could do instead, but that doesn't make it the right choice.
- Invite a colleague. If your concerns are about being on your own, then a bit of teamwork can help.
- Remember, just being there can give other people opportunities to promote you.

Tip 7: Seek out people who have a positive attitude

Positivity is infectious, particularly when it comes from someone you identify with

If you want a positive networking attitude, have a look around you at the people you consider to have one, or who you think are strong networkers. Try making a list of those people. Who on that list do you respect the most? Who has the most relevance to your networking aims or preferred approach?

Try asking them for a coffee and asking them about how they network, what they see as key to their approach, and how it fits into their work. Keep an open mind and just explore what works for them, looking for positive insights that you can remember and potentially use to feed your own inner voice a different diet.

If this conversation is successful, you could ask this person if they would consider giving you some mentoring advice from time to time, or even to coach you in the skills they have developed. Building this sort of relationship not only provides great ongoing support for your networking attitude, but in itself can help provide some of the framework and contacts you need.

If you are in a space where networking is proving difficult - and to be honest we all experience this at some time or other - then this person can be there to help you, encourage you and provide you with some ideas to get you out of the rut. You inner voice will, of course, be saying, "But they won't want to give me their time." You would be surprised how often people will say yes to an approach like this.

Keeping a networking notebook with occasional entries of positive points, successes and ideas gathered from these conversations can be really helpful in reinforcing your positive networking attitude after a hard day. This is not just about motivational quotes: it is about reminding yourself of the times you have been successful; the new ideas you want to try out; and interesting topics of conversation you have prepared.

Networking involves many other people and there are great opportunities to make your networking a team sport, working with your colleagues, supporting each other and maintaining each others' positive attitudes.

Prompts and ideas

- Identify people with a positive networking attitude and keep company with them.
- Feed your inner voice with a diet of positive messages and active people.
- Consider asking someone you feel is a strong networker to be a mentor or a coach as you develop your network.
- A networking notebook can be used to remind you of great ideas, key quotes and your own successes on the days where your attitude needs a top-up.

Tip 8: Stop reading this tip

Contact somebody you haven't spoken to for a few months

For most people, the greatest obstacle to achieving anything is procrastination in one form or another. You could even argue I am contributing to your procrastination habit by providing another networking tip for you to read, rather than actually doing some networking.

So in a few moments stop reading for a bit, and write down five people you haven't spoken to in the last three months who you feel you should get in contact with. Then add three more you haven't spoken to in the last six months. Number from the end of the list to the beginning and there's a simple list of eight people to contact with a priority based on time.

Next, for each person on your list identify something social or to do with business you know about them and write it alongside their name. Look at each subject: what do you know that could help restart your conversation with them? Can you research any information your company or firm have to help provide you with something to add to the conversation? Have you looked at their website or LinkedIn page recently? Once you start thinking about it, there are abundant clues available to you for how to pick up a conversation with them.

It shouldn't take longer than five minutes per person for you to come up with some simple starting points for a phone call or email exchange with them. You could even say, "It's been a while since we spoke so I thought I'd give you a call and find out how [xyz] was going?" Or, "How has business been since we last spoke?" This works better if you can mention when and where your last conversation was.

If you made no networking efforts yesterday, but today make just one phone call or send one email, you will have increased your networking activity by 100% in following up on one contact. Do this regularly and you will be surprised how many calls and emails come back to you, meaning you don't have to make that awkward call trying to reconnect.

Put this book down and do something to help your network now. Your good intentions will come to nothing without good actions.

Prompts and ideas

- Don't ask yourself, "Why should I do networking rather than read this book?" Ask yourself ,"What can I do for my network now?"
- Networking actions aren't always about going to events: you can get back in contact with people and you can make introductions to others without leaving your desk.

P.S. Remember to come back to the book afterwards ...

Notes

1. *The 7 Habits of Highly Effective People: Powerful Lessons in Personal Change* by Stephen R. Covey, published Simon & Schuster UK Ltd, 1989

YOUR
NETWORKING
STRATEGY

Why have one?

You have to deal with the fact that in business you are busy, or at least you hope you will be. Your time is often consumed by the delivery of your main business activity and involvement with the processes, support and financial administration required to do the job. A wide range of other short-term tasks can keep you occupied, enabling you to tick things off the 'things to do' list, and feed your sense of accomplishment.

A strong networking strategy, whatever your area of business, is about a number of business principles including:

- Direction: a clear sense of direction, what it is you are aiming to achieve and why it is important.
- Prioritisation: identifying the actions that move you along in that direction, eliminating 'low return' areas.
- Clarity: a sense of purpose and confidence in that purpose.

These help to provide motivation for you and clearer communication with clients, customers and colleagues.

Too often, networking is one of the tasks at the bottom of the 'to do' list, put off until all else is done and there is no other choice (which is almost never). A strategy helps you to focus on why you need to network, and the goals you will achieve; it will help you to ensure time spent networking is valuable and helpful, and that you are taking the right actions to meet your goals; and it will give you a clarity and purpose, which will come over to others creating a stronger, more memorable impression of confidence and professionalism.

Above all, a strategy will enable you to set, measure and chart *your* progress in building *your* network. Like any strategy, it will be a document in need of regular review and renewal, reflecting your achievements, changes in the business world around you; and other new factors that have emerged as you have progressed.

What will your strategy contain?

Of course this will depend upon you, on your goals, on your profession, on your business or employment status, and on the types of networking that suit you best. Below are some suggestions of things to consider in your strategy.

Goals and purpose of networking

Draw up a simple statement of your goals or aims for networking. This statement will provide you with a continual reminder of the personal goals and purposes you wish to achieve through networking. Throughout your career your stated goals and purpose will change and adapt according to what stage of your career you are at. You may be looking to build your reputation in an industry, or you may be looking for the next stepping stone in your career. As a result you will need to review your goals and purpose regularly, to ensure they remain relevant to, and motivating for your networking activity.

Segments

Your networking strategy may require different segments, and possibly different approaches to each segment. For example, if you work for a large organisation, part of your networking strategy will need to be about building your internal network and profile. Another segment may be about external networks, such as your approach to a niche part of an industry, or your specialism in technical expertise.

Targets

While a purpose is helpful, it can often prove too high level to be directly actionable. From the goal and purpose in your strategy, define targets for each segment. Your targets should be measurable, making success clearly demonstrable. As with your goals and purpose, your targets will change over time, so be prepared to revisit these, perhaps to set them at a higher level to challenge yourself further, or to amend them in the light of other changes in your circumstances.

Plans of action

Evaluate your targets to identify the actions you need to take in order to meet them. Are your targets about achieving new contacts or developing existing ones? Are they about gaining access to groups or speaking opportunities to increase your profile? Are they online or face-to-face based networking actions? Identify appropriate actions and then prioritise them.

Online

A key aspect of networking today is how you present yourself and interact online: blogs, social networking platforms, websites or providing your views in online forums are all forms of networking. You must consider the role that online networking will (or won't) play in your overall networking, and use online strategically to fit with your overall plans. All too often the approach of diving into social networking sites without considering why or how you are doing it, leads to an absence of helpful information and follow up. At the other end of the scale, simply ignoring the presence of sites such as LinkedIn or Facebook is no longer an option for the vast majority of us.

One way of developing your strategy is to look at it like a diamond (after all they are valuable). The diamond contains the different elements of your strategy and the actions associated with each area. This image enables you to look at the specifics in each sector whilst also considering the whole and its balance.

Example: Networking Strategy Diamond

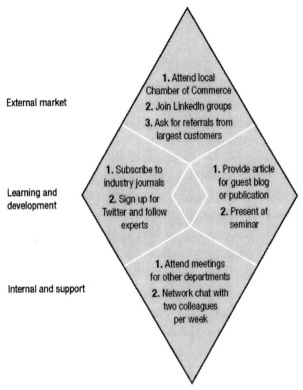

External market

1. Attend local Chamber of Commerce
2. Join LinkedIn groups
3. Ask for referrals from largest customers

Learning and development

1. Subscribe to industry journals
2. Sign up for Twitter and follow experts

1. Provide article for guest blog or publication
2. Present at seminar

Internal and support

1. Attend meetings for other departments
2. Network chat with two colleagues per week

The points of the diamond represent the different elements of your strategy, defined by your goal and purpose. In the example given, the central two points represent networking conducted around personal goals:

- Learning and development: improving your understanding, expertise and knowledge that you offer to contacts.
- Profile and reputation: increasing the range of people, internal or external, who are aware of you and the expertise you bring to your work.

The top half of the diamond is then concerned with

actions in the external marketplace, gaining new contacts, investing in relationships, speaking at seminars, or joining new groups.

The bottom half underpins the diamond shape as it represents the actions in the internal and support area as in, for example, getting to know the people in your organisation who you can introduce to others, or who help you to provide your services.

Some alternatives to these categories include having an online piece on the horizontal axis, which would provide focus to your strategy if developing an online presence was a key element. Instead of having the top half titled 'The External Market', you could be more specific and choose an industry that is a focus for you. The diamond shape may look different depending on the focus of your actions: if you have a strong focus on external marketing your diamond is likely to be tall with a wider base; if you are focusing on your own learning and development for career purposes, you will have a larger left-hand side in this example.

As part of your strategy you can prepare a diamond of your proposed actions and then see how this compares to the results you develop from your targets. This is a helpful visual to track the progress of your strategy and to consider whether your actions match the goals and purpose you have.

Using your strategy

Strategies are only helpful when connected to operations (in this case your strategy needs to be linked to your networking activity). When this is achieved, your strategy becomes an active operational tool. So here are some suggestions for how to achieve this:

- **Challenge yourself:** ask yourself some challenging questions. Am I focusing on the right things? Are my actions achievable and relevant to my aims and goals? Test out whether your strategy (to the extent you already have one) needs to change, and why it needs to change.
- **Make choices:** prioritise what you will do and the contacts or relationships you think you need to invest in. Time is precious and the act of prioritising will make you more focused.
- **Measure your success:** ensure you keep yourself motivated to progress your new or evolving strategy by measuring and celebrating your successes. Use the targets and benchmarks you have set for yourself to inform new, future targets. Be realistic, but keep stretching yourself.
- **Reassess and modify:** continually review your strategy, and look for how to keep it relevant and updated, based on what you have learned and achieved so far. You will be surprised how often your progress and your successes mean that you need to extend and modify your strategy.

Tip 9: Set an objective that works for you and your business

Do you want to have lots of short conversations, collect business cards, or will two or three quality conversations do it?

Part of your networking strategy should include objective-setting. At the macro-level, this will be about what your overall goals are: what you want to get out of your networking. In more detail you should consider your objective in every networking opportunity you have. What is it that this opportunity offers you, and what do you offer?

There are two main advantages to setting objectives for your networking. Firstly, the obvious advantage that your approach and work will be more focused. You will be prepared, serious about your networking, and clear on the value you want to offer others. Secondly, an objective takes the pressure off: once it has been achieved, you have the choice between continuing to network with the aim of achieving more, or getting on with other, non-networking priorities.

Context is important. You know your preferred styles of networking (groups, events, one to one, social, work-based and so on), and with experience you get better at knowing how to frame achievable, measurable objectives for that networking. You will know the context of the networking situation you are going to (big, small, formal, informal). The subject matter at the meeting or event will also impact your objective. In the context of the event, are you a learner, a reputation builder, or a subject expert?

Once you have considered context and the impacts you might aim for, be realistic in your objective. It is no help to you, your confidence, or your impact if you set yourself objectives you continually fail to meet. Conversely, though, don't make them too easy, or you will achieve nothing. Unambitious objectives may make the event comfortable and enjoyable, but when you come to assess the return on time invested, you will be disappointed.

You should be able to link your objectives for each individual networking opportunity to your overall networking goals and strategy. You probably don't have time to do this every time you have a networking conversation, but every two weeks or every month, stop yourself to ask whether the networking opportunities you have been taking are meeting the overall goals you have. Challenge yourself and be honest: it is too easy in networking to spend time doing the wrong things and end up with nothing to show for it.

Prompts and ideas

- Set an objective for each of your networking opportunities. Is this a new business, learning, reputation or personal goal you are contributing towards?
- Consider your approach, the context, and the subject matter of the networking opportunity, then set yourself a realistic objective.
- Ensure the objectives you set for each networking opportunity have a link to your overall networking strategy. Are you spending your time being a busy networker, and are you spending your time doing the right things?

Tip 10: Have the end point in mind

What do you want to achieve from this activity?

Most business relationships started with a networking contact point of some sort. It may have been an introduction through a colleague, a chance meeting at an event, a link-up through social media, or even sitting next to someone on a flight or train. The point is that networking is the activity that *starts* relationships. If you keep this in mind it will help at several stages in the networking discussion, but most of all it is a reminder that you are not finished just because you scored a business card or a meeting.

Starting with the end point in mind means thinking about and having a plan for what next. Rather than networking with the intention of gathering contacts and names, which you subsequently decide what to do with - or more likely ignore in the face of a busy working day - it is more about thinking why you want to know these people and what you will do to build a relationship with them.

A recent great example was when I worked with a tax advisory team, planning a series of seminars in the technology industry. In the period leading up to those seminars the whole team approached all forms of their networking with a goal of inviting people to the seminars, asking what they were interested in, and why they would attend a seminar. This approach provided an opportunity to tailor the content to the audience. In doing so, the whole team created warm contacts who were open to the information and ideas that would be shared at the seminars.

You can think about the end point you have in mind by asking yourself a number of questions:

- Do I want to increase general awareness next through publications and seminars, or am I aiming more specifically at an individual in the organisation, which will probably require a meeting or lunch with someone?
- Am I planning on a service-based next step (i.e. a specific offering or business issue to be addressed) or am I thinking of a more relationship-based approach (getting to know the individual better)?
- What timescales am I working to and are they achievable?
- If I want to move quickly to build the relationship with a particular contact, do I have the necessary offerings, opportunities and people available to make the appropriate follow-up?
- Is the end point about me or is it more likely to be introducing a colleague? If so, is my internal connection with that colleague strong enough to follow through?

Prompts and ideas

- A few minutes considering your aims and ensuring you have the necessary supporting information and people can increase the impact of a focused professional who can add value.
- Look to help: it may not be you who provides the answer, but you will be remembered as the person who knew someone who could.
- Lots of contacts and business cards are great, but what are you going to do with them? A business card without an end aim is potentially a waste of effort, or even worse, a contact feeling ignored.

Tip 11: Where are your contacts gathering?

Those are the events and places you should be — real world and online

In a recent conversation, I faced a challenging statement, "Networking is dead, everybody is connecting now instead." It was one of those moments in a conversation when my heart shouted *No!* then slowly my head confirmed that they were the same thing, just different labels.

I think my fellow conversationalist's point was that previous measures of networking such as events and business cards gathered are becoming less relevant, and that more technology-driven models have begun to dominate the scene. We debated this animatedly for a while, sharing a number of ideas and observations:

- Technology presents us with a new medium in which we can connect over distance and time in ways face-to-face networking has never been able to.
- In some service sectors, work is increasingly outsourced via online services, where high-quality digital portfolios are increasingly essential.
- Despite this, some face-to-face networking is still critical for many service-driven businesses.
- Often when we employ professionals, we like to have met them and ensured they 'fit' with us before we begin work.
- Credibility can be enhanced significantly through online activity in social media and blogs. Well-used, online activity improves the effectiveness of face-to-face networking.

- Different people and personalities have different preferences for the balance of their real world and online networking activities.

What was the conclusion? It was a useful discussion in which we both learnt different viewpoints. What we agreed upon was that the personal choice of where we network and connect is a key part of our networking strategy. As a result, if we are to maximise the return from our networking efforts, then we need to know where our contacts are meeting, what their personal choices are, and how to engage with them there.

For example, face-to-face opportunities such as business breakfast groups and technical seminars provide opportunities to engage with and experience meeting people. Online groups on LinkedIn provide forums for wider discussion with more people, and can continue conversations over longer periods of time. Real world meetings and online conversations merge when groups communicate online before, during and after a conference or event. Technology may be making real world more effective, but we *still* need to look for the moments and places where connection can start.

Prompts and ideas

- When preparing your networking strategy, look at the groups that are available on social media to see whether your potential contacts are participating in them.
- Identify the face-to-face events or groups that would be of interest: rather than trying to attend a wide range, make a selection that will feel focused and relevant.
- Consider starting either a LinkedIn group or a Twitter list to help you and your contacts exchange information and contacts more easily.

Tip 12: Choose your network groups

There's a finite amount of time, so be in a group to use it well

Are you looking for open networks (people willing to meet with everyone), or targeted networks (specific groups with targeted aims)? There are a wide variety of successful business networking groups varying in purpose, place, level of formality, tone, longevity (or novelty), hosting arrangements, membership criteria, industry, expertise and so on. There is no shortage of opportunities and each network addresses different needs and aims.

Membership network groups involve businesses or individuals who pay for membership of a select group which meets regularly to exchange contacts and business ideas. Often these groups are careful to minimise competition within the group by limiting the members to one per trade or industry. Members build strong links, an understanding of what each member can provide, and refer services to other contacts outside the group. These networks often involve opportunities to pitch.

Industry-based membership groups include chartered societies and institutes, royal societies, colleges and guilds. Such organisations usually provide a range of events (thought-leadership, training, surveys). The group or organisation often takes on a role as an advocate or mouthpiece for the industry sector. Networking opportunities are often built around professional development, for example CPD around meeting industry requirements and standards. Joining such groups may be dependent on working within that industry. Information is usually of high quality and attendance an effective way to build a profile within an industry.

Breakfast, lunch and dinner clubs can be membership or industry based, but many offer open invitations to a variety of businesses. Often locally or regionally based, these groups can be highly effective at reaching out in a given geographical area, and help form links between compatible businesses as well as reaching out directly to new customers.

Professional adviser hosted events usually involve a large number of invited representatives of companies and the attendance list is designed and managed by the advising firm. Attendees are often a mix of the adviser's clients and target contacts, and the adviser has created an opportunity to provide analysis or expertise on a given business area or industry as an incentive to attend.

Trade fairs and exhibitions provide the widest and most serendipitous networking groups, with a broad range of invitees and self-selecting attendees, and multiple potential reasons for attending. The challenge for the networker is finding the right people to talk to and being able to have a quality discussion with them.

Prompts and ideas
- Ensure you are clear on the goals of your networking.
- Pick groups or events that match those networking goals.
- Be clear in your mind how the events you are attending will deliver the contacts you want and the opportunities you seek.
- Consistency in participation pays off.

Tip 13: Are you using all available tools?

And which could work harder?

As we have established, your preferences determine the approaches you take to networking, and drive how you feel about the networking you do, whether you enjoy it or you see it as a necessary evil. But in today's amazingly connected world it is a racing certainty that nearly all of us are under using the available tools and networks.

Social media is a case in point. Many professionals from traditional sectors (accounting, law, education) are particularly wary of social media, for understandable reasons. Incautious comments made online have a habit of coming back to haunt us. But that is no excuse for not engaging. If your audience or network is using these tools, you have to understand them and find ways to engage that work for you.

It is worth paying a specialist to advise you. Our business recently took the plunge and paid a social media consultancy for advice. A relatively short consultation provided valuable information, insight and guidance. Most importantly, what the experience reconfirmed to me is how personal preferences can potentially be highly limiting. The consultants helped us review our wider networks and whether we were joining our different tools and audiences together in sensible, coherent ways. We also started to identify groups we hadn't reached out to for a while. Our resulting quick list looked a bit like this:

- Were we connected with our entire client and contacts network on LinkedIn?

- Did we engage with online opportunities around the conferences and seminars we attended?
- Were we connected through social media with our professional firm alumni from earlier in our careers?
- Did we have LinkedIn profiles for every individual in the organisation?
- Did the organisation have a good LinkedIn profile?
- Did we take advantage of all appropriate LinkedIn Groups?
- Did we do it consistently?
- Had we found everyone from our networks who was on Twitter?
- Had we evaluated their Twitter followings for useful contacts, as well as our own?
- What do we do with serendipitous business travel contacts?
- Had we linked up all of our social contacts with relevant professional interests into our professional online networks?

Based on this exercise we drew up a list of specific action points and allocated responsibility for them. We were astonished how much we learned from the exercise, and how many actions it created. You may well find the same.

Prompts and ideas

- Audit the networking tools and opportunities you use: are there any missing you feel should be there, and do you know why those that are missing are not being used?
- What tools are other people using in your area of expertise? Do you know why they are using those tools?
- External perspectives are illuminating. Talk to a colleague or friend in another organisation and get their view on your strategy and use of networking.

Tip 14: How good is your internal network?

Can people in your organisation link you up to key solutions for your contacts?

Whoever you are, however big or small the organisation you are part of, you have an internal network. (Yes, even sole traders have an 'internal network' of associates, service providers and 'friends of the business'). The health of that internal network is critical to the health of your external network and your ability to develop it. These two parts of networking are interlinked and without one, the other cannot be as successful. An external network that is not supported by an internal network is limited in the opportunities it can address and grow. An internal network without an external network has no new business to grow.

If you are part of a small practice or even self-employed you may be ignoring this tip, thinking, "This doesn't apply to me, it's only for staff of large accountancy, law or consulting firms." You would be wrong. Your internal network is about the range of services you can gain access to, and the people who are there to support you in delivering what you do. As a relatively small consultancy I often refer new and existing contacts on to other parts of my internal network of people I stay in touch with, and who provide complementary or supporting services to mine. This enables us to be helpful to our external network and clients by offering more than just our services but a range of other professionals in differing areas.

Your internal network comprises three parts: those who could sell your services; those you could introduce to your external network; and those who support your delivery, whether that be through subcontracting or providing support services in your organization.

So it is not just the people sat around you. Investing time in and building your internal network will help you to:

- Build your understanding and the scope of what you offer your external network and the business challenges you can help with.
- Communicate what you offer. It is incredibly difficult to make introductions or spot opportunities for things you don't understand, so internal networking builds your business development capability.
- Explore opportunities to work together and create new offerings for your external networks by collaborating with others who have similar goals but different skill sets. Collaboration can provide you with new ways to approach opportunities and problems.

Prompts and ideas

- Ensure you balance the development of your internal network with your external network; and don't become overly focused on one to the exclusion of the other.
- Understand your internal network as more than just the colleagues sat around you. It should comprise all those who help you to sell your services and all those who support you in delivering services.
- Work with your internal network and put effort into building your mutual understanding of each other. The act of collaboration will help to build the possibilities and the trust you have in each other.

Tip 15: How far can your network reach?

Have you ever asked anyone for a referral or an introduction?

We often overlook the easiest routes to success. For many years businesses, professional service firms, charitable bodies and many others have used customer relationship management approaches and systems to maximise the use of their contact data to identify new possibilities and leads. So we can take a similar approach to networking, starting by looking at the people and relationships we already have as a source of new relationships.

For example, you can choose to look at your existing network in a number of ways:
- Sector or industry based
- Internal or external to your employer
- Client, supplier or partner based
- Work and social.

Within each area, who do you already know, and have you asked them to introduce you to someone? Being able to see people's LinkedIn networks, Twitter followers, and Twitter follow lists makes this far easier than it ever used to be. The art is in knowing how and in what way to ask the question. Over coffee? By email? Telephone? You need strong relationships in your network to know how to judge the answer, which will vary in each case. Your contacts with reciprocal networking attitudes will be happy to introduce someone they trust and believe is relevant. Others may be more risk averse and be happy to broker contact, but without implying approval or endorsement. Be willing to accept any help and introductions you are offered - you can take it from there.

Not only are referrals easier to ask for than generating relationships from cold contacts, they also make relationship building easier. People are more open to introductions from the people they already know or trust than they are to approaches from strangers. It can be a more acceptable form of networking for many than event-based networking.

Of course referrals are much easier when you are already recognised by your network as someone who gives back, and when you are someone who willingly and helpfully provides endorsements, referrals and introductions. All of us are more likely to be helpful to people who have been helpful to us. This isn't bribery or, "You scratch my back, I'll scratch yours." It's about networks and people supporting each other.

Prompts and ideas
- Asking for introductions from people you already know is an easier and more productive option than meeting new people cold.
- Review your network in sectors, clients, work and social areas to see if there are people who could introduce you to others.
- Be helpful to others in sharing and introducing your network, then others will be more willing to be helpful in introducing you.

YOUR
PERSONAL
IMPACT

Personal Impact

We all have an impact: the impression we leave behind on others that forms their opinion of us. You know you have a personal impact, because you will have formed opinions about the impact of pretty much every other person you have met - so it stands to reason that other people do the same about you. Your personal impact on another may be the result of first impressions or, more likely, the result of consistent meetings and discussions.

When talking about others we use a lot of headline words to describe their impact. For example, 'honest', 'entertaining', 'loud', 'boring', 'interested', 'enthusiastic', and so on. Sometimes we remember the details that led to these impacts and we are able to build a narrative such as, "He/ she is very enthusiastic, they talk with a great deal of honesty about their business in the recession. They can be a bit loud when making a joke ..."

The more important the 'people' parts of your business

or role are, the more vital your personal impact is. You make a lot of impacts in the first 30 seconds of meeting someone: these initial impressions are often strong and they are gradually altered over time, or reinforced. It is much easier to build on a good first impression than it is to amend a bad one. Your personal impact is the sum of people's experiences and impressions of you.

Where does impact come from?

Visual impacts: what people see

Visual impacts are created without you saying a word, and stem from a wide variety of cues: your body language, your hairstyle, attire that is appropriate or inappropriate, whether you are constantly checking your phone. If the other person can see it, it may well be contributing to your impact. Before you open your mouth, you have already given out multiple signals about how much you care for your appearance, whether you feel comfortable, and your level of interest in others present.

Vocal impacts: what people hear

It isn't just what you say, it's how you say it. Intonation, volume, speed of speech, and the use of pauses and silence, are often referred to as the music of our voices. In terms of impact, the music of your voice gives out multiple messages such as how important or interesting you find a subject or a person, and your confidence - or lack of it - in a conversation or an opinion. It can reinforce or undermine the substance of what you are saying. Think for a moment: when was the last time you heard somebody saying one thing, but at the same time you thought they *meant* another? As listeners, we subconsciously pay as much attention to *how* people say things as to *what* they say.

Verbal impacts: the words you choose

Your choice of vocabulary; the level of jargon; whether you speak concisely using clear language; the number of fillers (*um, er, you know, like ...*); and your ability to tailor your language to your audience, all create impacts. Your ability to tailor your choice of words, and the tone of their delivery, is often your most noticeable verbal impact. Many of the best professionals and business people have an ability to express what they want to say in a succinct and interesting way to anyone. There is real art in pitching your choices of language and metaphorical frames of reference in ways that will engage the person or people you are talking with.

Touch and gesture: context-appropriate and respectful contact

In business, touch is most commonly experienced through a greeting or a parting handshake. In some contexts and cultures it may be a kiss, and in others any form of touch may be taboo. In multicultural, multifaith workplaces, it is more important than ever to be alert to when and where the handshake or its equivalent is appropriate. You can communicate many different messages and feelings in a handshake: we have all experienced the limp, damp handshake, and the handshake so firm it seems to be demanding submission. Touch and gesture are part of your personal impact so they are well worth paying some attention to. If you are travelling and networking abroad, seek advice from people with experience of the region about the culture of greeting and exchanging cards.

Yes, smell too

As we have established, so much of our impact is about non-verbal cues, the hardwiring of our brains, and social conventions and taboos. Whether we realise it or not, we all register when someone else smells good or bad. So don't go to a networking meeting straight from the gym. Keep a toothbrush at work or in your bag (and use it). Don't go for overpowering perfumes and colognes because they can be as much of a repellent as bad odours. This is all about common sense, so make it usual practice.

How others experience your impact

Other people experience your impact through their senses and then through how they filter and process that sensory information, and that is also how you experience them. To understand how others experience your impact, you need to understand how you experience theirs.

Visual impacts usually come first: you observe people approaching you, joining your circle, and people standing around who you intend to approach later. The signals you receive will then be processed through the internal filters that tell you what you think and feel about others. These filters include:
- Prior experiences. Does this person look like

somebody I recognise, and if so who and what did I think of them?
- Expectations. What or who do I expect to see in this group of people or in this meeting or in this room? Does this person's appearance meet my expectations and if not what does it mean to me?
- Comparison. How does this person's appearance compare to others in the room, either those I can see or those I have already met?

Next comes a close contest between hearing and touch, depending on whether the person you are greeting gives an introduction or a handshake first. All of these stimuli create a strong impression very quickly. Then, once someone begins to speak, your brain applies a whole new set of filters:
- How interesting and interested does this person sound?
- Based on the questions, statements and tone used you will judge how much you want to listen.
- Can I listen to this person easily? If someone's voice is too fast, quiet, mumbling or monotone it becomes very easy to just switch off.
- Is this information useful? Depending on the language and content you are hearing, you will begin to distort, delete and generalise to suit your own frames of reference.
- Am I being engaged in conversation, or talked at?

Can you affect your impact?

There are a number of unseen ways you can affect your personal impact: through awareness, understanding your own preferences, being prepared, adopting a positive attitude and through understanding the difference between intention and perception.

Awareness

Just increasing your awareness of your impact is a significant step in managing it, adapting it and, most of all, using its strengths to build contacts. A lot of time can be focused on the ways you can change your impact, but it is equally important to *recognise* where you have succeeded in achieving a positive impact.

Awareness can be achieved in a number of ways, the most common being feedback from others. This can be very hard to gain in the initial stages of contact building, but if you are working with or networking with a colleague you can have a conversation beforehand to set up the opportunity to observe each other and give feedback.

Alternatively, many training courses provide role-play training, including recording and reviewing interactions. This kind of training takes courage to sign up to, but the rewards can be immediate and highly effective.

Understanding your own preferences

I have written a lot about preferences, and I will continue to do so. Each of us has personal preferences – which begin to be hardwired into us from a very young age, meaning that certain behaviours feel more comfortable and natural than others. Knowing how and where you feel comfortable is an extension of your awareness. By being aware, you can work on expanding the range of contexts where your impact can be maximised. Seeking out situations and opportunities where your preferences will help you to maximise your impact will enable you to feel confident and comfortable when networking.

Psychometric tools such as Myer Briggs MBTI, Saville Wave, or OPQ 32 can be really helpful here, but be sure to get feedback from someone who understands the tool you have chosen and can link it to your own particular experiences.

Being prepared

Preparation can provide confidence. Your head knowing and your heart telling you that you are ready for a given situation nurtures your confidence, and this feeds into your behaviour enabling you to:

- Be more concise and clear in what you are saying.
- Approach people with enthusiasm.
- Deliver an introduction that supports your value.
- Be willing to talk about a range of topics, business and social.
- Reduce signs of nerves such as fidgeting.

Later on we will look at the balance between the right amount of preparation and becoming obsessional. Preparation should help you have a positive impact, not take so long that you don't get to the networking.

Adopting a positive attitude

Your attitude, or state of mind, has a significant effect on your impact. A bad day, or a difficult conversation, can dampen down the positive and accentuate the negative. A good day, or a recent success, can do the reverse, amplifying your attributes and mitigating negatives. So it is obvious - but often overlooked - that ensuring you arrive at networking events in the right frame of mind is important. If you are not at your best, you need to choose the technique that works for you in order to shift your mindset, be it taking time out from your day to relax, going for a short walk, listening to music, reading something motivational, watching a TED talk, or sharing your woes with a colleague. However you do it, you need to get those troubles or concerns compartmentalised and off your mind before you network. Arriving in a frame of mind that is you at your best allows you to make a good impact.

Intention and perception: there is a difference

A key to flexing your personal impact is grasping the difference between intention and perception. You may want to come across as welcoming, friendly and interesting. Your mind and your thoughts may well be telling you that's who you are and what you want to do.

Unfortunately, the perception of your personal impact is built by others and felt by others: your behaviour is passed through *their* filters. Therefore you need to know the impacts you want to make and understand what behaviours convey those impacts to others. If you want to come over as interested, then showing signs of listening through relevant questions, paraphrasing and eye contact will all contribute; but checking your phone will not. You need to match your actions to your intentions.

Tip 16: What is the impact you want to create

What does that look like?

Your impact is created by your range of behaviours and responses throughout an interaction from beginning to end. We have been looking at the component elements, so there are two key questions for you to answer:

- What is the impact you want to make (described in simple words)?
- What does that impact look and sound like to others?

Identifying or naming the impacts you are trying to create through the course of an interaction is helpful. To start with you might want to be seen as 'welcoming', 'enthusiastic' or 'open'. During the course of the interaction, the initial impression might develop into being seen as 'interested', 'interesting' or 'focused'. And the end of the interaction is every bit as important as the beginning. As the conversation is wrapping up you might want to be remembered as 'proactive', 'helpful' or 'friendly', or all of the above …

For each of these words you can then begin to think of the behaviours you need to demonstrate to achieve that impact. Some of the words will feel strongest for you and others may be more challenging. For example, 'welcoming' probably includes:

- A polite introduction and welcome.
- Asking about the other person early in conversation.
- Establishing eye contact.
- A confident but not aggressive handshake.

Someone who is interested in a conversation will use

questions to find out more, linking what the other person has said to their questions, thereby demonstrating active listening. Usually this will include eye contact to show attention, appropriate nodding, and gestures indicating recognition. Often people in an engaging conversation will 'lean into' the conversation or stand closer together than they might otherwise.

Thinking about your impact is not rocket science, yet it is all too easy to forget to pay attention to it, switch off, or tune out, and then be surprised by the reactions of others.

Prompts and ideas

- The impact you want to achieve will vary according to the context, the type of work you might want to be doing and the people you are meeting. Think about what impression you want the other person to be left with, and prepare yourself to be able to deliver it.
- Identify the behaviours that indicate an impact you wish to achieve. Think about other people you know who have that impact: what do they do and say to create it?
- Identify the invisible factors (e.g. preparation, positive mental attitude) that will help or hinder your impact.

Tip 17: What are your eyes saying?

They tell others where your attention is directed

In most western cultures, eye contact is the start point of our impact and the signals we make to each other in any interaction. Correctly or incorrectly, we all form opinions about what others are thinking based on the eye contact we receive.

When you are networking, you want people to know you are interested in them. You want them to share information with you or to listen to what you have to say. This reciprocal atmosphere is fostered by your non-verbal communication: your body language, of which eye contact is a key part. It is often said *the eyes are the window to the soul*, and whether you believe in the soul or not, yours are a signal as to what is going on inside.

You use your eyes to signal when your attention is moving from one person to another in the group, or to solicit feedback or response to a comment. There are a variety of ways in which breaking eye contact for prolonged periods will create an impression of disinterest, including:

- Looking over someone's shoulder for another individual such as a friend, a colleague or a long-term client.
- Looking at your smartphone or mobile device to check if there are any updates.
- Reading materials for the meeting, presentation or event.

- Looking towards a different area of the room, for example where the drinks are served.
- Looking at someone else in a group when you are being addressed by someone.

Your use of eye contact should show you are interested in the conversation, and, even more importantly, the individual. Breaking it for too long does the opposite. If you aren't interested in talking to someone now, don't be too surprised if they don't talk to you later about a piece of work they have.

It can pay to be aware of people who are not engaged. You can spare a glance around the group from time to time to check if others wish to be more active, or just to check the visual signals of their opinion on the conversation. Helping people who are struggling to find an entry into a conversation can be an excellent way to foster friendships. Use your eye contact to provide positive signals to others, to draw people into discussions and also to observe the dynamics of a group discussion.

Prompts and ideas

- Remain in the conversation until it's done. Keep eye contact with the people you are talking to: they are the most important people in the room for you during that conversation.
- Reduce distractions by putting your phone out of reach or putting down any reading materials you may have.
- Share eye contact around the group of people you are talking to, and do this naturally as the conversation moves.

Tip 18: Jargon only tells me which books you have read

Speak clearly, concisely and avoid peppering your conversation with acronyms and jargon

Numerous volumes have been written about management speak. Some have been very good at encouraging people to be simple in the points they make and to speak clearly and concisely. Others have increased the range and usage of terms which many of us find baffling. The courses I run are a great source of feedback about what is currently hot in the world of management speak. Here are a few of my favourites: *it's our burning platform at the moment; we could run a few ideas up the flagpole; we need to consider the blue sky options; we're super-excited by this idea; this is at the bleeding edge.* I am sure you can add to this list, or have perhaps indulged in some management-speak bingo in the past.

There is also a proliferation of TLAs (three letter acronyms) within many corporations. I recently attended a conference for a large consulting company and realised that for the majority of the presentations I hadn't understood a word, for the simple reason that they were littered with unexplained phrases and acronyms. A skilled colleague from the firm managed to summarise the presentation in a few simply worded points.

In professional contexts there is a huge temptation to try to sound interesting or important to others. We often do this by expanding our language or using new terms we have heard from others, rather than just sticking to the point. The impact of this behaviour is often the reverse of its intent. Rather than looking interesting we manage to create confusion, or even worse leave them feeling insulted or patronised through a lack of clear language. We may also raise a suspicion that there is little substance behind the facade.

Sticking to concise points helps to make the information and value we are offering much clearer. In a competitive marketplace being the person able to convey complex issues in simple terms can be a real and valuable differentiator. Rather than using management phrases it is often more powerful to use an example or story to illustrate a point or problem, because narratives that assist understanding are memorable.

A good test is to challenge yourself with the following question, "How much of what I am saying would be understood by people in this business, regardless of their position?" If you are delivering technical expertise it is unlikely the answer would be 100%, but the higher the percentage, the easier you are making it for people to know your expertise.

Prompts and ideas

- Limit your use of management expressions, and where possible explain what you mean using an example or story.
- Seek feedback from clients or colleagues on how easy you make it to understand new concepts or ideas. Feedback is your opportunity to open your eyes and ears to how you come across to people.
- Ask your friends what they do in their work and role, and see if you can understand the explanations they give or if you catch them using management expressions and TLAs.

Tip 19: Your impact shapes your personal brand

Feedback helps you know what that is

Your personal brand is about how you would like people to see you, what messages you would like them to take away, how you would like them to feel about interacting with you and, importantly, what they would say to others about you. It is well worth spending a few minutes writing down some key words or phrases that describe how you intend others to experience interactions and conversations with you. Look for the recurring themes: these are likely to be your key values. Begin to think about how other people would understand or experience the words you have chosen.

What your contacts say to *other* people about you is part of *your* personal impact. Finding out what they say is a measure of your impact and of whether it truly reflects your personal brand. One of the best ways to do this is through feedback, although seeking it requires a degree of bravery. It is never a lot of fun to ask someone what they think about you. The risk of hearing something you don't like is obvious, but just as importantly, many people struggle to listen attentively when they are being given praise. Soliciting and listening to feedback requires trust. Start with some of the contacts you have known the longest and ask them for some feedback on your impact and see if they are willing to share their insight. These questions may be helpful:

- What do you remember thinking about me in our first conversations or meetings?

- How has that changed or developed in our business relationship?
- Have you any specific examples of things I have said or done that have affected your impressions of me?

Be warned: if you ask these questions of people you have just met, then you will get some strange looks and potentially very bland answers. It would be a fast track to creating a bad impression, so select people to ask for feedback carefully. You want people who are willing to be honest - positively or negatively - and able to give you some examples.

Feedback data is helpful. Look for themes in what people say about you:

- Where does your impact come across positively?
- Is this in line with the words you use to characterise your personal brand?
- Where are the gaps between what you want people to feel and understand about you versus what they actually do say about you?
- Consider how you can close that gap through changes in behaviour, increased levels of awareness or improved preparation ahead of networking.

Prompts and ideas

- Identify the key words you want to describe your personal brand: what five characteristics would you like people to be focusing on when they talk about you to others?
- Seek feedback on your impact: how a person experienced you when you first met and how that has changed in the course of your working relationship.
- Compare your aspirations with the empirical feedback to identify where there is a gap and what you can do about it.

Tip 20: Does your handshake measure up?

We all know the impact of a bad handshake

Your handshake is one of the first experiences people will have of you. It is a very personal one too. That first physical contact affects different people in different ways: some find it intimidating, whereas others seem to regard it as a competition. Have you experienced any of these?

The Bone Crusher when the person shaking your hand appears to be conducting some form of strength contest. Generally speaking, inflicting pain never supports a good personal impact.

The Wet Towel when you shake the other person's hand only to find it's wet - presumably with sweat - which makes for a very uncomfortable experience. (Note: if you are prone to sweaty hands, the problem is *not* improved by wiping your hand on your clothes. Whilst it may be less wet, if I've seen you wipe it, I really don't want to shake it.)

The Finger Shake when a handshake the other person offers is just the front half of their fingers, and the hands never fully engage. This can be seen as a sign of nerves, a reluctance to meet, or aloofness.

The Politician's Glove which is the double-handed handshake, meaning you are unable to extract your hand until they release it. This commits you to a longer handshake and for many it will feel insincere or driven by another agenda.

Too Long - women are often the target of this, when a man holds on to the handshake for too long, making the woman feel uncomfortable, embarrassed or bullied. If your work involves networking with members of the opposite sex (and it is rare for it not to), making them feel uncomfortable is not going to be a winning strategy.

A simple handshake, offering the whole hand and shaking twice will suffice (of course you can't control how the other person offers their hand, but you can take your part properly). A handshake is a greeting and should put people at their ease through the brief, initial, equalising contact. Anything more is unnecessary and uncomfortable. Good handshake etiquette is:

- Maintain eye contact with the person you are shaking hands with and give them your full attention.
- Greet the person by name and introduce yourself (if this has not already been done for you) as you shake hands.
- Ensure you have completed each handshake before breaking eye contact and moving on to someone else.

Like almost everything in life, a good handshake can be practised, even if that seems like a weird idea. If you work in a group all of whom need to network professionally, it is worth having a practice session.

Prompts and ideas

- Ensure you give people your full attention when shaking hands: this is a key moment when you have each other's full attention.
- Remember: eye contact and a verbal greeting.
- Practice makes perfect: enlist help.

Tip 21: What is your online impact?

Beware: it is all too easy to appear blunt or judgemental online

In the same way you have to consider your impact in a face-to-face situation, it is vital to have thought about the impact you want your online profile to achieve. What messages do you want other people to take away when they visit a website you are on, your LinkedIn, Twitter or Facebook profile, or the blogs you contribute to? There are more similarities than you might think between our online impact strategies and our face-to-face techniques, visual and verbal.

Visual images and video are an ever-growing aspect of online engagement. You can share images of yourself, visuals relating to concepts you like, slideshares of presentations you have given, or even videos you have made or appeared in. These all contribute to the overall impact you make, illustrating how you see the world around you, what is important to you and, of course, how you look. If your profile picture on a social networking site is in a tie and suit it sends a different message to a picture of you relaxing (with pets or skiing for example).

Whenever you contribute to discussions, share updates, provide blogs, and so on, you are giving *verbal* indications of your language and your credibility. People reading what you say will form an opinion about whether your contribution - and therefore you - is interesting, misled, dull or controversial.

There is a third point linked to verbal contributions. In online environments we engage in discussions that other people are able to observe. This is unlike face-to-face networking, where it would be very strange to have a sizeable audience. This means that online the way you engage in discussion and the things you say can have impacts on a group of people you may never have met. So you need to be aware that what you are saying and contributing could be more public and more permanent than it feels in the moment.

A danger in networking can be to separate the face-to-face world of networking from online. In many areas there are significant overlaps and the process of building a relationship will involve both environments at some point in time. Be prepared to consider your impact in all networking environments and be prepared to act to adapt it.

Prompts and ideas

- Determine what you want your online profile to say about you; not just the words you use but what the reader will think and feel after visiting your page.
- When contributing to online discussions bear in mind that the audience and participants of the discussion may be wider than those you can see in the thread of the discussion.
- Ensure any visual images you use online reinforce the impact and profile you want to have and do not dilute the work you do elsewhere.

YOUR
PREPARATION

Why prepare?

There are many great one-liners about the role preparation plays in networking. I particularly like, *Fail to prepare, prepare to fail,* which, like most terse but astute observations, over-eggs it a bit, but conveys a core truth. The point is that if you can't find the time, effort or motivation to prepare for something, then you shouldn't be too surprised when you don't achieve the results you want. Preparation is about improving our chances of success and so applies to networking, the same as everything else.

Think about the last time you felt unprepared, be that a meeting, an event or a simple catch-up over coffee. Was that a comfortable or uncomfortable feeling; one that helped to improve or impair your performance? Obviously the scale of the meeting or event will have an impact on how much you felt it mattered, but even in light-hearted contexts most people rarely enjoy feeling uncomfortable.

Many people approach networking as something that 'just happens' in their work or social life, without any preparation or need for it, accepting whatever results they gather from this approach. Unfortunately, this means they are wasting a lot of precious time because:

- They are attending events that are unlikely to meet their networking goals (or what would have been their networking goals had they bothered to articulate them).
- Their social networking profile tells people nothing about them, and displays only a lack of interest.
- They are unprepared for conversations of interest to contacts, to the point of even being unprepared to fully discuss the subject in hand.
- They turn up to the wrong place, or the right place at the wrong time.

All such problems, ranging from simple administrative oversights to the negative impression, can be completely avoided with a modest amount of preparation and just a bit of awareness of who will be there and what they are likely to want to talk about.

When it comes to personal impact, preparation is key to enabling most people to feel sufficiently confident to network effectively. Like everyone, you have a threshold or minimum level of preparedness that makes you feel comfortable enough networking, be it at a business meeting, a less formal catch-up with a client, or a big event. It is important to develop enough self-knowledge to learn what your threshold is for each context. Preparation provides you with a bedrock of relevant knowledge that helps you to come over as focused and credible in conversation with others. This allows you to feel calm, which is expressed in your body language as you approach others and engage in conversations.

Preparation also informs the intelligent questions you will ask, not just the statements you make or facts you will offer. It is often those questions that make more of an impact than any assertions you offer. Finally, your preparation gives you direction, enabling you to connect with contacts in a way that feels action orientated and customer focused. You will come over as clear on the next steps and how you would like to continue the relationship, and in doing so the other party or parties to your conversations will be far more likely to want to reciprocate and continue contact.

The role of preparation is therefore to give you the best return on the time you have invested, and to present the best view of who you are for new contacts.

What can you prepare?

So what can you prepare? Clearly you cannot prepare for everything or all scenarios, but a little bit of thought can identify some quick wins. If you are attending a business meeting with a client or customer, the content you need to prepare in advance will be implicit in the agenda (and if there is no agenda, ask for one or suggest one). But above and beyond that, you can also ask yourself some questions to enlarge the scope for additional discussion:

- What is changing in their business and industry at the moment?
- What are the non-agenda subjects they are likely to want to express their views on or ask your opinion about?
- Who is going to be there who may have a different

view on these subjects, or may have a different role in the business to the people you have met before?

- Do you know what interests these people outside of work? How can you build the rapport in this relationship further?
- What research will they have expected you to do?

If you are going to a seminar, conference or a networking event the questions above are still relevant but there may be some others to add. For example:

- Does the advance programme information tell you who is attending, who is speaking and any details on the presentations? If delegate information is not published in advance, it can be worth asking for it.
- If you know who the attendees are, have you decided who you would like to meet and looked at their business website to research their business? The same goes for speakers of course.
- If the speakers are 'big names' and you want to summon the courage to talk directly to them it can help to know what motivates them outside the business world. They may be the patron of a charity, have a cause they champion, or have a particular passion for an obscure hobby.
- If you can't obtain a list of attendees, try working out who is likely to attend, and what their interest in the event is.
- What are your views on the subjects of the presentations? Of course these may well develop and adapt as a result of what the speakers say, but knowing your opening position is never a bad idea. In what depth would others expect you to have a view or opinion?
- Do you know anything about the venue and the hosts

(corporate host or otherwise)? Knowing something about them can be an easy way of providing useful contextual information to others.

In all networking, there will be moments when it is *not* appropriate to talk business - perhaps after you've had a bit of focused discussion that has run its course. It is important to be up to date with current affairs, what's in the news, the arts and theatre can prove useful ground because not everyone wants to talk football. It is an ongoing act of preparation to be aware of what is happening in a range of social spheres, including news, arts, culture and sport. There are now so many sources of free media to draw upon, news feeds for current information, newspapers and their websites for articles and analysis, so there really is no excuse not to keep reasonably up-to-date. But remember, it's not an exam, you're just gathering up resources that may prove useful.

You should always have your introduction prepared, but the best introductions have been thought through before they've been made. (*See page 122* for advice on greetings and conversation openers.) Consider what you want to say about you, your expertise and your clients, ensuring that it is relevant to the context you will be networking in. Thinking these things through before a networking opportunity is a lot easier than trying to work it out in the moment you are shaking hands.

How long should preparation take?

It would be very easy to say as long as you feel is necessary. Clearly there are factors affecting the answer to this, such as your comfort threshold, the number of people you expect or want to meet, the subject of the meeting or event, or the level of knowledge at which it is pitched (introductory through to expert).

Any preparation is helpful, but don't overload yourself. It is not about becoming the expert on everyone in the room and what they want. It is about feeling comfortable to start discussions and see where they go. You need to exercise some pragmatism and prioritise what research and preparation is likely to give maximum return on time invested.

I find that 15 minutes preparation will improve my knowledge and confidence in any networking situation, and once I go beyond 30 minutes I begin to worry about how much I will remember. So my optimal time is between 15-30 minutes. It is well worth establishing your own minimum and maximum boundaries; thereby optimising your time effectively.

Tip 22: Who do you want to meet?

And where can you find them?

This tip occupies crossover territory between strategy and preparation because it is about making sure you are going to the right places to meet the right people. Participants in our networking courses often ask us, "How do I make sure I am talking to the right people or the people I want to?" One of the answers to this is to ensure you are going to the right places to meet them.

An output of your strategy work should have been an understanding of what type of people you want or need to meet. If you can identify individuals all well and good, but it may be in the form of knowing the role descriptions, level of expertise and of course the industry or sector. By formulating this description, you can begin to determine some possible meeting or networking places by identifying similarities or common needs. For example would they attend:

- Industry-based events run by an industry organisation where they can gain training and share best practice?
- Expertise-based seminars provided by their advisers where new information on technical matters is on offer and where they can compare practice?
- Conferences or exhibitions to meet new suppliers or customers or to gather new ideas.
- Local organisations such as Chambers of Commerce or business round tables, where they can refer business and discuss more local business issues.

This list may well imply some intermediate actions you must take to enable you to gain access to the right group, through membership or introduction, or you may need to subscribe to an industry body before you are able to meet the right people. The effort will be worth it and will save you the wasted networking time at inappropriate events meeting disinterested people.

If you already have contacts who belong to the organisations or groups you want to be part of, you have a great opportunity to be introduced to the group and referred at the same time. By discussing your aims with your contact, you may be able to make mutually helpful introductions, improve your relationship with your existing contact, and gain access to networks that are a strategic match for you.

Once you have attended a group for a little while, be honest in assessing for yourself whether this networking is meeting your needs. If you are not meeting the right people, go back to your strategy, try to identify why not and then look for new groups or places to meet these people. Regular reappraisals to check or confirm you are putting yourself in the right places are well worthwhile.

Prompts and ideas

- Ensure your strategy helps to identify who would be the people you want to add to your network; and try to describe them as specifically as possible.
- Ask yourself where these people go to network. Some of them won't, but many will, so where would they go – industry group, conference, advisers, online social networks or social events?
- Ask your existing contacts in industry or local groups to make an introduction for you, utilise their access to the network and achieve additional credibility by being introduced by somebody they already know.

Tip 23: Find out who will be there

Then ask yourself why

Before any meeting, event, social gathering or project workshop it is always helpful to have information about who is going to be there. You will feel more relaxed knowing a few names. It is even better if you recognise some you know already. You can prepare with a little research about relevant individuals (remember we are talking light research here, not stalking).

If you are the host of an event or part of the hosting organisation, you will of course have access to the proposed attendance list (never a guarantee that everyone will show up). The fact that most of us now have portrait photos on networking platforms, company websites, blogs and articles means it is now much easier to know what the people you want to meet look like. If you are hosting the event you could go a stage further and brief your team with a picture board of the attendees. There is nothing like being greeted by name and having your badge handed straight to you for making an impression.

When attending open events such as conferences or training courses it is often far harder to get a list of attendees. You can ask the organiser but there may be reasons they are not keen to release this until the day of the event or conference. This may be due to the likelihood of it changing or even a promise not to release names to participants. It never hurts to ask, rather than missing an opportunity through a failure of imagination. If the organiser is not prepared to give names, try asking -

without making a nuisance of yourself - if they can tell you the companies represented or the organisational responsibility and role levels they are focusing on in promoting the event. Taking a thoughtful look at how and where they are marketing and promoting the event will give you a lot of clues.

The question, *why?* is your failsafe fallback. *Why* are people attending *this* meeting, event, seminar, conference or workshop? You can think about the answer to this from a number of angles:

- What value or output might they be looking to gain?
- What compliance, CPD or other responsibilities might they be fulfilling through attendance?
- What personal and business goals will they contribute to by attending?
- Who might they be looking to meet?
- How might they describe their reasons for attending to other people?

Everyone has reasons for showing up - not just you. Some of them sound more positive than others (development, meeting new people) than others (compliance, instructions from a superior). In simple terms, no reason, no show.

Prompts and ideas

- Wherever possible obtain an attendance list in advance.
- Think about why people are going to this event or meeting, either collectively or for specific individuals. Consider what it is they are trying to get out of the occasion.
- Remember when you are there that everyone has a reason for coming along, otherwise they would not turn up. We all have a lot of other things we can do if we don't believe this is a good use of our time.

Tip 24: Use all available resources

There are plenty of ways to gather context-appropriate information in advance

There are many who will say they like to 'be flexible', 'go with the flow', or even 'just see what happens'. Fine if you are confident enough and sufficiently well informed to sound interesting and credible in almost any situation and on any subject. The majority of us are not blessed with that level of confidence, so preparation gives us the information and knowledge we need. There is a big difference between the impact you make when making it up on the spot and when you are being open to the ideas and potentials of a conversation, and that difference often lies in the preparation. Moreover most professionals have pretty well-tuned baloney detectors.

You have a huge range of resources at your disposal. These are some of my favourites:
- The BBC news website and feeds (for current affairs and some subject-specific information).
- Economic comment from "Big Four" firms, provided in free emails from their economics teams.
- LinkedIn and Twitter (to identify an individual's specific interests, experience, expertise, authored content and personal interests - to the extent the latter are shared in public).
- Industry-based journals or websites (to provide industry-specific insights).
- Free newspapers available locally or nationally

(*Metro, Evening Standard, Business AM* and so on) for interviews or unusual stories.

- Company websites for press releases or news on latest developments.
- Colleagues and people already within my network (for information on their experiences with companies or people).
- Venue information from websites or marketing data.

Target your preparation to increase your confidence ahead of networking. If you are going to a meeting or working on a client project then you can afford to be very specific in your preparation, focusing on the company and the people involved. When attending an event or conference your preparation may be more about delegates, conversation openers, or your understanding of the subject under discussion. You will learn what makes you feel comfortable in advance and can refine your preparation methods accordingly. I aim to have five key points (be they on individuals or general topics) that I can have for networking, which enables me to prepare without getting swamped. Just try now to see if you can list five topics of conversation you could take to a general networking event or social evening tonight: you will be surprised how easy it is.

Prompts and ideas

- Prepare for the known and potential topics: you'll feel more confident and the surprises will be, well, less surprising!
- Don't mistake being flexible for being unprepared: preparation is the key to being flexible. Without it you're just making it up.
- Aim for a number of points that you can easily recall from your preparation. Do not do so much you overload yourself, otherwise the time is counterproductive.

Tip 25: Do some homework

It pays off – whatever the subject of the meeting, seminar, workshop or conference

Unless you are super-human it is highly unlikely you already have an interest in or an opinion about absolutely everything. Having said that, it is pretty simple to have a view on the topic of the meeting, workshop or conference. After all you already know the subject(s) at hand. When networking it is disappointing to encounter someone who clearly is not interested or motivated enough to engage in relevant conversation. It is also rather rude to show up uninformed, and it is unlikely to pass unnoticed by the very people you want to engage.

If you are attending a meeting, then there is an unwritten code of conduct that says you will do your preparation, read the agenda and bring along any supporting information you can contribute. These behaviours form an appropriate spirit in which to attend a meeting. This expectation is amplified if you are attending an event, conference or workshop and your expertise is in the area being covered.

So take enough time to consider:
- What are the subject areas being raised and discussed?
- What is my view on these areas?
- What experience and (shareable) stories do I have to offer to support my views?
- What are my key questions?

- What questions might others reasonably expect me to be able to answer?

There are a number of reasons why you might not do this preparation. Age-old excuses and their counter arguments include, "I was too busy to review the invite and subject matter." If you are so busy you can't prepare, why invest the time in attending an event looking unprepared? Or there's, "I want to know what other people think." However, conversations are a two-way activity, so whilst great networking does include being interested in and listening to others, if you are going to ask for their opinions and information you need to be sufficiently well informed to ask intelligent questions, and in response be prepared to offer your own views. This is also known as *give to get*. Please don't give me, "I don't think I have anything interesting to add." You don't need to be saying something people have never heard before: it is about demonstrating your willingness to engage. Being an expert is not required, but you do need to demonstrate your interest.

Prompts and ideas

- Do your homework on the subject areas involved: others will expect you to, and if you don't your impact will come over as less professional or as disinterested.
- What will be the attendees' interests in this subject area, and what are their likely questions?
- If you turn up without a view or an opinion to give, don't be surprised when nobody is interested when you do eventually have something to offer. Remember, *give to get*.

Tip 26: When did you last Google yourself?

Everyone can do their networking homework, so check what internet searches offer up about you

A statement of the obvious perhaps, *but* you need to know if there is a disconnect between what you are working hard to project, and what a search engine turns up about you. If you are a serious networker and have engaged online in a well thought through manner, there will be plenty of on-message information about you out there. But even if you are relatively inactive online, you may be surprised about how much is out there about you.

It pays to ask friends to do experimental searches for you too. Internet search is not user-agnostic, and search algorithms mean the order in which search results on yourself are offered to you is not the same as for others. (Another excellent reason why you need someone who understands social media in your internal network.)

Access to the internet is now so ubiquitous that if you are not using it well, it marks you out as unprofessional. There are many web-based tools and services at your disposal to help create a positive impact to new contacts. This doesn't just mean using the internet for research so you can demonstrate how interested and credible you are. It also means knowing what the internet is telling other people about you before and after you have met them.

I am not just talking about removing inaccurate, unattractive or outdated information. Getting information removed can be time-consuming and difficult. A more fruitful strategy can be to push the poor information down the search rankings with up-to-date, current and well received content. This is your opportunity to position yourself appropriately, for example by:

- Ensuring your business networking platforms give up-to-date profiles that actually say something about you. (If I have taken the trouble to search you up, then I'd like a reward on that effort please.)
- Posting regularly in group discussions or forums in your expertise or industry area. Building credibility online converts into opportunities offline.
- Using blogs to write your own articles, or possibly to guest write for business sites. Self-hosted blogs consume considerable amounts of time; by collaborating with others you can reduce the burden.
- Checking that your personal networking is not in conflict with business networking goals. This involves clarity on why you are using sites such as Facebook, LinkedIn, Twitter and Instagram. Look at what you are sharing in the personal and business space, and ensure it doesn't compromise any of your goals.

Prompts and ideas

- Audit your online presence. What platforms are you currently working on and are you using them in a way that is designed to achieve a networking goal for you?
- Search for yourself online regularly, keep a note of the top hits and check whether they are what you want to be known for.
- Blogs can be time intensive, so consider whether you could guest write for someone else's blog that matches your aims, expertise or industry. Look to collaborate with others.

PART 3

The GLAD Approach

GREET

The greatest challenge

The biggest hurdle many of us face when we are net-working and making new contacts comes in the first few moments: the greeting. This is the challenge I hear more about than any other through the surveys and the courses I run.

This feedback comes in a wide variety of statements and questions. Do any of these sound familiar to you?
- How do I break into a group?
- I haven't got anything valuable to say.
- I haven't got anything in common with people.
- What do I say to start a conversation?
- They are so much more senior than me, they won't be interested in me.
- How do I introduce myself professionally?

For many people just saying hello, making an introduction and getting the conversation started with someone new can feel intimidating, full of uncertainty and risky. The sense of risk is elevated by perceived or actual differences in levels of seniority, experience and age, gender, and a lack of confidence in ourselves.

The reality is almost always far less scary than your over-active imagination and inner voice are telling you. Conquering the fear requires you to remember the other person is just another human being. You must be willing to make an effort on their - and your - behalf. You will often share a common purpose with the people you are looking to network with, so don't fail to make enough use of that purpose. If you are in a meeting or a workshop for a project or engagement, then you are already working towards a shared goal, be that an IT project, a legal matter, a financial proposition. Your shared goal is a ready-made reason for, and lead into, new conversations. At events, conferences and seminars, people have come either to gain new information from speakers or to make new contacts and network: both are great reasons to risk a conversation.

If your inner voice is giving off messages that make greeting new people difficult for you, then remember the same is also true for many others in the room. Never assume you are the only person in the room who is nervous about meeting others: the majority of people have some degree of trepidation. Some embrace it; others let it defeat them. This book is all about not allowing yourself to be one of the defeated.

What can you do to make it easier?

The things we have already talked about

Your positive networking attitude will mean you are in the right frame of mind as you approach others and introduce yourself. Your networking strategy will help you to be in the right place, meeting the right people, and therefore coming over as someone of value and with a purpose. Keeping your impact at the front of your mind will ensure that others get the best of you, see you at your most positive, and take away the impressions of you that you want them to. Finally, your preparation is your kit bag of tools for networking. With it, you are walking into a conversation ready for what it will bring.

Prepare your introduction(s)

You are *your* specialist subject, and you could possibly talk about yourself for hours. That is not the point of an introduction, though. Work out what is the key information other people need to have to begin having conversations with you. Your introduction for each context or group of people will be slightly different, because your introduction is not just about you. It is about you *in the given context*, and in relation to the people you will meet. Over the course of time, you will gain increased experience and expertise to include in your introduction, for example new projects, new clients, or new industries can all provide additional introductory material. They key is to keep it brief and relevant.

With more networking practice, preparing your introduction will take less and less time, and you will become sufficiently confident to adjust your introduction whilst at a meeting or event. Context-appropriate adjustment is good, but it doesn't eliminate the need to prepare. Get into and maintain the practice of thinking about your introduction in advance, build your confidence and know that you have introductions that work.

Pick the right people to talk to

When you arrive at a meeting or an event, take a few moments to observe what is going on. You may have been on body language training courses and read management text books on managing and interpreting body language. All of us will have experienced or exhibited the body language of a person who does, and a person who does not want to be talked to. So look around, observe what signals people are giving and respond accordingly. If someone is in an animated and private conversation (clues include people leaning closer in to each other, with feet pointed towards each other so they are facing, and people who are animated in their facial or vocal expression), then do not disturb that conversation unless those involved give you a signal to join. Look for the signs of people open to new discussions, those who are stood shoulder to shoulder, making eye contact with people around the room - maybe you - and those who are on their own and not occupied.

Be polite

Under the pressure of networking it can be tempting to believe you need a great phrase or one-liner to start the conversation or to break into a group, when in actual fact all that is required is courtesy. So for a group, "Do you mind if I join you?" is all it takes. Even if this is met with a negative response such as, "I am afraid, this is a private conversation," you can express your apologies and a desire to speak later on at the event.

Remember to let them know your name as soon as the opportunity presents. Include, "My name is … "

with your introduction. Then as soon as possible, turn it around to show an interest in them: we all respond better to someone who is polite to us; courtesy inspires reciprocity.

Above all else, be you

Do not try to be someone else. So often I have seen people try to make grand entrances, be bolder than others in the room, push their hands into others and shake hands very vigorously. I have watched people being greeted in this way step back, try to find some new personal space, look uncomfortable and seek another conversation as soon as possible. In fact - precisely the opposite reaction to the one that was sought.

A greeting should be a positive experience for all parties, so that includes you: by feeling confident and positive about yourself, you will convey your confidence in your greetings and other interactions. Believing in yourself makes a better experience for all concerned.

When networking, people want to know who *you* are so give them an insight while they are in *your* company. Let them work out if the well prepared, well informed you is someone they might want to build a business relationship with. If you pretend to be someone else, they will pick up on this, and will feel less inclined to trust the reality (if they get as far as discovering it).

Don't get hung up on it

From time to time, greeting somebody new will not go as well as you had hoped. You may stumble over your introduction or they may not respond with much warmth. This happens from time to time for a whole variety of reasons, many of which will not be anything to do with you. Just remember that impact and networking are about building a relationship and while it is great to have a good start, there is plenty more to do, so all is not lost.

If you stumble over your introduction, move on quickly with a question, such as, "And what business are you in?" or, "How's your day been so far?" This will get the conversation going, allowing you the chance to listen to the other person, giving you a moment to recover. You can then follow up with a supplementary question, or if you have recovered your equilibrium, venture a comment on what they have said.

You may be having a very difficult day; we have all had them, and we try to push on through hoping nobody notices. It is okay to give yourself a networking break if you feel you aren't going to be able to give of your best. This is clearly harder when the networking is part of your normal or required working day, in which case stick to getting the job done and don't give yourself extra pressure. If it is an event, think before you go, "Am I in a suitable frame of mind and is my preparation adequate for me to make the best of this?" Occasionally you may decide that you would be better off not networking today. Avoid giving yourself a hard time, just be honest and ensure you are in a better place for networking next time.

Sometimes it is not about you. Your new contact may just have had a difficult day or phone call. They may be thinking about something outside of work that is troubling them. Jet lag is a common reason for people feeling very sub-par, and being empathetic can win you a friend. On one occasion when someone I was networking with confessed to jet lag, I agreed networking was quite hard work in those circumstances, to which they said they would rather be at home. We exchanged cards and agreed to have a coffee a few days later. Out of an act of friendliness and empathy, I gained a much longer conversation.

When another person is preoccupied, empathy can go a long way to building new relationships, drawing them into networking conversation. If your greeting is received with lower energy than you expected, don't assume it is about you. Use your powers of observation to try to work out what is going on.

Above all, be kind to yourself, don't get hung up about your greeting, because it's all too easy to get to a place where you don't want to network, or where the pressure of those first few moments with new people becomes a barrier you can't overcome. To build your network, you need to meet new people so even when some greetings don't work out, don't give up. Keep meeting and greeting people: the good experiences will outweigh the bad.

Tip 27: Aim to join open conversations

Body language, eye contact and levels of animation are all clues

Choosing who you want to start a conversation with carefully is important. Spending a few moments observing the room is a valuable investment in identifying people who want to talk, who are open to meeting new people, and who are the contacts you want to meet. Avoid the temptation to walk up to the first person you recognise.

Everyone gives out signals about how they are feeling, particularly about whether they want people to join them or not. All you have to do is read those signals. Often the most certain indicator of a willingness to talk is sustained or regular eye contact. Not just a fleeting look and then look away, but eye contact that catches yours. This is often combined with a change in facial expression which indicates recognition of your presence.

People's body positioning will give you useful clues. Those who stand in an open position to each other, for example shoulder to shoulder as opposed to face on, are often subconsciously leaving room for someone to join them. A pair of people face on to each other are often indicating that they do not wish to be interrupted. The volume, pace, and variety of a conversation (the animation) will also tell you whether people are deep into it or if it is still at a welcoming level that can be joined. Quieter face-to-face conversations are often indications of private discussions, whereas laughter and humour may be a more relaxed scenario to join.

As well as the signals people transmit, you need to keep in mind who *you* want to talk to (you know because you have done your preparation). See if you can recognise them, and approach them. If they are busy, find a way to alert them to your interest in speaking with them. Showing you are interested is much better than saying afterwards, "I couldn't speak to them, they were busy."

It is often tempting to stick to your most important customer or client, and I am not about to advocate ignoring them. But you need to balance this with your networking goals. Will talking to your existing client help you to achieve them? Might they make referral-style introductions for you? You may have something you wish to discuss with them, but is it best to make a separate arrangement to meet with them? After all, you already have a business relationship.

If you are part of a large firm hosting an event it can be even more tempting to catch up with friends and colleagues. Again, you have existing relationships. If you talk only with colleagues and established clients, you will only leave invited guests wondering why you didn't speak to them.

Prompts and ideas
- Take the time to observe people: everyone gives signals about when they are willing to talk.
- Choose the right people, balancing your need to speak to specific individuals with the openness of people in the room.
- If you want to speak to someone who is busy, flag it up to them.

Tip 28: No stalking

It is off-putting and will kill the opportunity

Walking up to a stranger or someone more senior can be nerve-racking, and for many people this is exacerbated by group situations. The behaviours resulting from your nervousness may make you much more hesitant or tentative. This can look like:

- Walking very slowly towards people, occasionally stopping.
- A reluctance to speak and ask to join conversations.
- Fleeting eye contact, scanning for a friendly face.

When you feel nervous or hesitant, your intention is not to impose yourself on the conversation, and not to appear too aggressive or too fake in your enthusiasm. However, from the other point of view it doesn't look like you are hanging back out of politeness; it just seems a bit weird. "Who is this person hanging around our conversation? They've been there for a bit now? Are they waiting for me to say hello?" Unfortunately it is all to easy for it to look a little like you are stalking a group of people, waiting for the weakest one to cave in and ask you to join them.

I hear about this problem from many delegates on my courses, particularly those who are taller or shorter than average. For those who are taller it can often feel like they are peering into a group or leaning over someone's shoulder. For shorter people it can be hard to make the required eye contact. Counter-intuitively, the only solution - for people of all heights - is to be a little bit bolder:

- Once you have decided who to talk to, walk up to the group confidently, signalling that you want to meet these people.
- Remembering your manners is all the next step takes: "Excuse me, do you mind if I join you?"
- Make eye contact long enough to say hello and exchange names.
- Take time over your name - not too exaggerated, but clear and slow enough to be heard.
- Shake hands, not just your fingers, and not for too long ...

Hanging back and hovering on the margins may be motivated by caution and politeness, but the resulting behaviour is irritating and confusing. Once you've walked into the room, it really is a case of nothing ventured, nothing gained.

Prompts and ideas

- Aim for welcoming as an impact. It doesn't need to be over the top, but you need to say through your non-verbal language that you want to be there.
- Be proactive: if you want to talk to people then act like you do, not like you are being forced to do something you dislike.
- Look at the space available in a group: people who are very close together may be engaged in animated or private conversation, so may not appreciate a new joiner.

Tip 29: Do as you would be done by

It is common courtesy

We like to be treated politely and to be shown respect by others. A desire for respect and courtesy are culturally embedded in human societies, of all creeds. This is why the, "Do you mind if I join you?" approach is so powerful. In all networking scenarios, the same rules of politeness and courtesy apply as elsewhere. Yet I often observe people marching straight into groups, introducing themselves loudly and over confidently. Instead of seeming impressive, they seem rude.

"Hang on," I can hear you say. "Just one page ago you were telling me to go up to groups of people boldly," and indeed I was. The difference is in tone, manner and nuance. People who march into groups probably think they have a great impact. But it is simply rude when the interruptor has not taken the time to read others' body language, or find an appropriate moment.

Whenever I approach an ongoing conversation, be it at work, down the pub, at the football, or out with my family, I always ask if it is okay for me to join. That simple phrase, "Do you mind if I join you?" gives other people choice. It allows the people having the conversation to flag up to me that this is a private conversation, and it immediately communicates to them that I am respectful of them. The question can produce many responses ranging from, "Can you give us five more minutes, we just need to finish this conversation?" to, "Not at all, please do." The key is that I respected others' right to a choice.

When others do let you join in, they will often tell you what it is they are discussing. Or, once you have introduced yourself, you could ask what it was they had been talking about. Again, you are giving them choice, rather than imposing yourself.

Be aware that people don't always verbalise unwillingness. If there is any uncertainty, too long a pause before an answer is forthcoming, or if people give visual clues of wanting to keep the conversation private, be prepared to say, "I can see I interrupted you, hopefully we can speak later," then make a polite retreat. Often, when people have asked for a bit of time, or when you have sensed that you chose the wrong moment, and withdrew, they will then come and seek you out, which always makes for a positive start. They have approached you on their own terms, ready for a change of subject.

The success of, "Do you mind if I join you?" reconfirms something else we have already covered: you don't need great one-liners; just courtesy. Politeness tells people a great deal about what it would be like to work with you.

Prompts and ideas

- Just because it's networking time doesn't mean you should start approaching people any differently from normal.
- Be prepared to be told the conversation is private; you can always ask if you could speak to them later, then look to join somebody else.
- Note the body language of the people you are looking to join, this will give you signals about whether they wish to engage with you.

Tip 30: Negative responses are nothing to be scared of

They are opportunities to find out why, what if, or what else

As we have established, one potential response to the, "Do you mind …" opener is, "Yes, we do mind," (which although it says yes, is a negative response to your question). It is the potential for this response that stops us asking whether we can join a conversation or provide an input to the conversation. The real trouble with this, and the reason why many people are so scared of it, is that it feels *really* personal. Of course there are all sorts of valid reasons, none of them about you, why the answer might be no. So avoid the temptation to leap to the conclusion that it is about you.

As you struggle in the moment to deal with an answer you neither wanted, nor really expected, you can come across as awkward, a bit inarticulate, or at worst embarrassing. And of course a negative reply might not only come at the start of the conversation - it might be in response to a subsequent question. Whenever it comes, 'no' can impede your progress and sap your confidence unless you know how to deal with it.

Firstly, it's unusual for someone just to say 'no' to almost any question in a networking situation. It's a pretty blunt response and is more likely to be embedded in an explanation. Secondly, if someone has said 'no' to a request or a question, then try to think how you could understand more and possibly why they have said 'no'. If you choose the right kind of open or interested but probing question, you can explore the negative response without coming over as direct, blunt, challenging or defensive. For example you could try, "That's interesting. Please could you tell me how [why] it is different [the case/not the case] for you [your business/your clients]?"

The fear of 'no' can stop us going into conversations or asking questions where the answer may be no. And the result of that is banal, low-level conversation that never explores anything of note. But turned on its head, 'no' can be your opportunity. When asking to join a conversation and being met with a negative reply, you could respond, "I'd like to talk to you later if that is possible, would there be a good time to come back?" or ,"Would it be okay to call or email you in the future to arrange a better time to meet?" If your initial approach is polite, it will rarely be stonewalled.

At the close of a discussion or conversation, 'no' can still be an opportunity to develop a better response. For example, if you suggest a follow-up action only for it to be met with a 'no', you can try, "What would be helpful [would work] for you at this point in time?"

Prompts and ideas

- 'No' can mean several things, so ask questions to understand what it means for your contact, and thereby develop a better response or approach.
- Remain open to the answer 'no': it isn't a rejection. People have to decide they want to say 'no' before they do, so continue to run the risk of 'no' as a reply: you are likely to learn more.
- Try open questions to open up the discussion: 'no' is an answer to a closed question, and you may not have intended to ask one.

Tip 31: Your introduction can start the conversation

So provide more than just name, rank and serial number

Your introduction is the first information you give when meeting someone, so why limit it to the stuff they can already learn from your name badge and business card? Your introduction impacts people in many ways including, "They sound interesting," through to, "That's nice." If you have aroused interest, it will most likely lead to conversation. "That's nice," on the other hand, is a typical response when people don't know what to say, perhaps because you sounded dull, or didn't create the possibility for a response.

There are three levels of introduction you can offer when meeting someone new. It can sometimes be helpful to think of the metaphor of juggling with some tennis balls.

Tennis ball one: who you are (name, rank and serial number). This introduction reiterates your business card. You have given your name, the company you work for and your job role there. But in the tennis ball metaphor for the person you are meeting, it is a bit like watching you juggle a single tennis ball: boring to watch and no opportunity to join in.

Add in ball two: who you are and what you do. You are offering a little more, aiming to explain what it is you actually do (you need to bear in mind your audience and be able to explain what you do, whilst still sounding and feeling valuable). You now have a couple of balls in play:

easy, but a bit of thought required. As there are two balls in play, it could become participative. You can throw a ball to someone by starting a conversation based on a link or a question.

Tennis ball three: who you are, what you do and how you help. At least three tennis balls are in play here: you, what you do, and the value it delivers (and possibly for whom). Doing this successfully requires some preparation, as you need to be able to clearly and quickly describe what it is you do in terms of the output or impact others experience. By introducing the third ball you are creating more possibilities for links and questions.

The third ball introduces the power of a story. All human beings respond to stories: it is how we are wired. Your narrative makes you more confident, as it is the recounting of experience rather than iterating your name or position. For the listener, your story provides many more opportunities to build a conversation, ask questions about you, your story, the business you helped. Stories engage: we identify and empathise with them much better than with business cards and rank.

Prompts and ideas

- Draft a range of introductions for you, based on the deliverables and outputs you provide to customers or clients.
- Once you have drafted your introductions, try them out on colleagues or friends. See what questions they would have.
- Treat the introduction as the opportunity to start a conversation, so throw those tennis balls, and see who is up for a game of catch!

Tip 32: Remembering new names is challenging

So develop some memory techniques

Remembering people's names in the first few seconds of meeting them can be a real challenge, and one that terrifies many of us. When you network, your mind may be so full of all of the tips and advice you have been given that you forget to listen. Of course others may be just as nervous, speak too quickly, or have a name you find hard to pronounce.

It really is all about focus. The result of all of your hard work and preparation is this moment of greeting, and not only are you greeting a new person, but they are greeting you. You need to be relaxed enough to focus on them, listen, and hear how they greet you.

There are a number of easy things you can do that help fix a new name in your mind:

- Repeat the other person's name as early as possible in the conversation, and make a point of using it at least twice. Doing this helps imprint it in your memory.
- Associate the person's name in your memory with something or someone you already know. For example, if they work at a company where you already know someone, try to link the two facts in your memory by saying to yourself, "Sarah works at ABC Ltd, so does Peter" or, "Teresa worked abroad in South Africa, as I have too."
- Facial recognition – research shows that many of us remember names by noting facial features or appearances, then creating associations in our

memory. For example, hairstyle, glasses, scarves and ties can all be helpful prompts.

We all sometimes forget names quickly, so don't be afraid to ask someone to give you their name again. This can feel embarrassing to do because it feels like an admission of failure, or a suggestion that they are unimportant. But think about how you would feel if someone else had to ask you. You wouldn't hold it against them, or mark them down as incompetent. You would repeat your name to them because you know exactly how difficult it can be to remember lots of new names at once.

There are also some simple things we can do to help others remember us. Speak a little slower when saying your name. Wear your name badge in a way that makes it visible: if it is under your lapel, on a shirt or blouse under your jacket or, potentially embarrassingly, on your belt, then it is a worthless accessory. If you put it on the right hand of your jacket or shirt, your badge comes more clearly into view as you offer your right hand in a handshake. Wearing your name badge visibly and readably is good meetings and events etiquette.

Prompts and ideas

- Make links between people's names and memorable facts, either about them or associations they have with you (holidays, prior employers, clothing).
- Use visual clues to help you remember their names, facial characteristics, appearance, voice and so on.
- Do not be afraid to ask if you have forgotten their name, assuming it's not the third or fourth time. Very few people are offended, and they may well take the opportunity to check your name too.

LEARN

Conversation is a great learning opportunity

When you meet a new contact, whatever the scenario, you have a fantastic opportunity to *learn* more about them, and to begin to build a relationship with them. For both of you there are almost endless potential benefits that can be created by sharing knowledge, ideas, experiences and opinions. Therefore this section on learning about others offers you more tips than any other section of the book.

Once you have done the hard work of getting into a good position to meet new contacts, and you have taken the step of greeting them, you can begin to reap the benefits, build relationships and have a long-lasting positive impact. To do so, you need to demonstrate a willingness to engage. You need to show interest in others, in their knowledge and experience, and in what they have to say.

Every conversation is a learning opportunity. If you don't recognise it as such, you may come over as disinterested or insincere, or worse that conversation is a chore and you are just filling time. So what opportunities *are* there in a conversation? The list is endless …

Learning about your new contact

Your first conversation is a great opportunity to learn more about your new contact. Your greeting and initial exchanges will have helped you to learn each other's names, and probably your roles and places of work, or the organisation you are representing. Conversation is an opportunity to take that knowledge further, learn more about each other, your organisations, your roles, and each other's views on a range of subjects. You can begin to investigate the potential for common interest or shared opinions.

Building the relationship

A conversation is an opportunity for both parties to gain an idea of what it might be like to work with each other. By its very nature, two-way conversation is a collaboration. By sharing views on a range of subjects, you both gain insights into how you might interact as customers, clients or suppliers. You can develop the beginnings of a rapport that enables you to explore how a business relationship might benefit both parties. Conversations are opportunities to identify shared areas of interest, compatible skills and knowledge. Remember, when you are networking, you aren't looking for people made in your own image.

Developing credibility

The questions you ask and the statements you make build - or destroy - your credibility. You demonstrate your understanding, or lack of it, of your business area, your customers and your client industries through the questions you ask, and the relevance of those questions. The additional opinions and/or knowledge you offer demonstrate how that credibility may turn into value for your new contact as a customer, client or colleague.

Developing contacts

Your networking conversations put you in contact and build links with people whose company you can enjoy. Not all conversation is business-oriented, and the opportunity to share non-work related interests can be a relaxing and enjoyable part of your working day. Taking an interest in what motivates others, and the things they enjoy doing, enhances your network.

Knowledge building

In addition to learning about a new person, you have the opportunity to expand your own knowledge through the expertise they are willing to share. So there are potentially learning opportunities, new information and new perspectives to be gained, just by being willing to strike up conversations. Together, you can extend the boundaries of each other's knowledge, and even develop new ideas or approaches.

Profile building

The conversations you have when networking build your profile in two ways. Most obviously, you build your profile with the person you are talking to, but you also give them the opportunity and the material to talk to other people about you. Therefore you are building the potential for profile within their network as well.

What impact do I want to build during this conversation?

All of the activities above contribute to your personal impact, so it is worth keeping in mind what impact you are aiming to achieve, (you have already thought about this). What impressions are you trying to build in others' minds, and what words would you wish them to use when thinking about you later on, and possibly when describing the conversation you have had to others? Depending on the nature of the event and networking goals you have set for that event, your aims for your personal impact may vary. However, many of your aims will be consistent. Indeed to come across as authentic in your networking, there needs to be a consistency about your personal impact. If it is too variable, you risk developing a reputation as a maverick, and not reliable.

Impacts and ways of achieving them

Engaged and engaging

Coming across as engaged and engaging is achieved through your ability to engage in conversations, both social and business, in a professional manner, by showing courtesy to others, respecting views, and knowing when to add your opinion (and when not to).

Credible

You demonstrate that you are credible through the depth of your knowledge in your area of expertise, through your responses to the subjects others introduce into discussion, and through giving thoughtful responses. You can be a great conversationalist without appearing credible in any area. Credibility arises out of the depth of your knowledge in combination with the thoughtfulness with which you apply that knowledge.

Knowledgeable and experienced

You can demonstrate your knowledge by referring to examples and case studies. Where you have direct experience, you can include narrative content (being careful never to share confidential experience).

Energetic

How you appear and how you sound indicate your energy for the subject under discussion: you give clues with both your body language and your tone of voice. Changes in voice, tone, and intonation draw people's attention to your passion or knowledge, and your body language supports this through facial expression and animated hand gestures. As with all networking, there is a lot of nuance, and a fine line lies between being energetic and being too boisterous. Be self aware, and build your awareness through listening and feedback.

Interested and responsive

Listening is a big part of coming across as interested and responsive. We all unconsciously recognise the body language signs (eye contact, nodding, recognition moves, verbal endorsement) of someone who is listening, and listening properly is both a powerful networking tool and a rare skill. When you listen, you are able to ask questions that follow on directly, relevantly, and intelligently from what someone has said to you, or volunteer information that endorses and enhances what they have said. If you have listened, you can summarise and check what you have heard from other people, and they are often delighted to have their thoughts paraphrased back to them intelligently: it is a form of personal validation.

Warm and friendly

Your tone, facial expressions, handshake and eye contact all do the work here. In fact, almost everything you do can show whether you are really interested in meeting and getting to know someone. Another person's impression of your warmth for them, and your friendliness, will be directly related to how interested they feel you are in them.

Get curious

Use your networking attitude and the preparation you have done to 'get curious' about people. It is a mindset I have come across in conversation with lots of great networkers: they are keen to know you, what's happening for you, what delights you and what bugs you. They don't do this because they have attended courses, or because they have read great books. They do it because they want to. Being genuinely, but tactfully, curious about other people is essential to developing your network.

Style and type of conversation

One of the key areas I cover in my workshops, and in the tips that follow, is the style and types of conversation you will have when networking. Many of us have a tendency to focus on either personal and social conversation, or on professional discussion, finding it hard to blend the two. A surprisingly large number of people believe that they are capable of only one kind of conversation, or that others will be interested in only one or the other. In fact it is exceedingly rare for someone to be so one-dimensional that all they want to talk about is one particular subject. Depending on a wide range of variables, most people can and do cover a whole range of conversation types on any given day, or at any given event.

The environment in which we are networking is usually a key determinant of the style and type of conversation that will be had. In the office during work hours, it is fair to assume that business-based conversations will predominate. If we are catching up with a business contact over coffee, the conversation may still be business-focused, but is likely to be less formal and less constrained in the subjects covered. At a business seminar, discussion is likely to be based around the theme of the seminar and will therefore feel quite focused. However at evening events with a more social agenda, conversation is generally more relaxed and social.

The conversations you have at any given event may end up covering a wide range of topics, and it is impossible to know all of them, or be prepared for all eventualities. So in your preparation, you need to make some good judgements on the most likely ones, and then rely on your networking attitude to keep you flexible. What is currently in the news about sport, culture, arts and music will influence the kinds of conversations you can strike up. Similarly the business and current affairs news may naturally move the conversation to a more business-based focus. What is happening in the world around you directly influences the available conversations.

You can also use your eyes and ears to see how others are reacting to what is under discussion, and then use that data to inform your responses and how you steer the conversation. You can win a friend for life by subtly steering a conversation from a subject that someone is finding difficult or embarrassing.

Three easy rules for getting the style and type of conversation right:
- *Think* about what type of conversations the people you are networking with are expecting to have, given the context.
- *Watch and listen* to how others respond to conversation topics.
- *Have the conversation they want to have.* Respond to the outcomes of the first two rules: don't just analyse, use them to inform your choices about how you participate.

In short, focus on others, and on what they want to talk about.

Tip 33: Ask open not closed questions

Open questions help you to learn about the other person

There are countless courses, blogs, and theories on questioning techniques. Questions are a fundamental part of two-way communication, influencing, and connecting, so it is no surprise they turn up everywhere.

The value of an open question is clear: open questions invite people to open up with their opinions; to share their ideas or experiences; to identify the links between you; and creates an atmosphere of shared interest. You want to learn more about the person in front of you, their business, their interests, and any issues or areas you could help with, so you need them to talk. Closed questions will draw the odd word, and maybe confirmation of some facts, whereas an open question allows your new contact to take the conversation wherever they want to, and to share as much as they want with you.

Useful open questions for networking include:
- Tell me more about ...
- What do you do at ...?
- How do you see ...?
- Please could you expand on that for me?
- What are your thoughts about ...?

Closed questions tend to occur in a networking conversation for two key reasons. Firstly, nerves when starting a conversation may result in questions beginning with, "Did you ...," "Is it ...," or "Was it ...?" Taking a little more time to relax and phrase the question better always produces a better result. For example, instead of asking, "Did you have a busy day?" try, "What's kept you busy today?"

Secondly, and more dangerously for networking situations, the unconscious motivation behind a closed question is a desire for the other person to confirm a point of view. For example, "Do you think ...?" or, "Is it the case ...?" can imply, "I think - and I think I'm right." This second type of closed question will close down the conversation, as it tells the other person that you are more interested in your own opinion than theirs.

If you want to offer an opinion as a conversation starter, then follow it with an open question. This puts your idea and thoughts into the conversation, then openly invites a response and a counter-opinion. For example "What's your view on that?" as opposed to "Do you agree?" The latter question forces either agreement or contradiction, whereas the former implies an openness to different viewpoints or opinions. It is a more emotionally intelligent conversational technique because it demonstrates your interest in the other person and your acknowledgement that they may not necessarily share your opinion.

Prompts and ideas

- Take the time to phrase an open question. A pause doesn't say you've got nothing to add, it says you're thinking carefully.
- If you have a view, try making it into a question: "My experience is [succinct description], what's yours?"
- Where possible think up some subject-relevant open questions ahead of any client meeting, event or workshop.

Tip 34: Offer easy conversation starters

Great networkers make easy conversation

"How's your day going?" or, "What drew you to this event?" are perfectly acceptable: you don't need complex, entertaining, or deep conversation. Easy openers help the people you are meeting, because people enjoy conversations they find it easy to be part of, and this draws them to you. Conversations don't go from nought to sixty in seven seconds.

Avoid the temptation of what feels like a high impact question. For example "How do you see the European Central Bank's stress tests affecting economic behaviour in the UK?" may sound clever, intelligent even, but starting with such a complex question is far more likely to deter people and make you look like you are trying too hard, or are arrogant. The art of conversation is making others feel comfortable enough to share their thoughts and ideas, not scaring them off.

Identify some easy questions or opening conversation starters that others will find easy to answer and you too will find it easy to have an opinion on. For example:

How's your week going? People may offer what has been occupying them and give you an opportunity to explore either a business or a social topic with them.

What drew you to this event? People have all sorts of motivations for attending events, so this is often a great starter for conversation. For example the person you are talking to may know one of the speakers, or have a particular problem they are hoping the event will solve for them.

How was your journey? A classic question for many networkers, because getting to places on time given the pressures of work, and the complexities of transport provides us all with plenty of anecdotes plus the opportunity for a touch of humour. For me this has worked as a starter in any group in any country. We seem to share a desire to tell and hear travel stories and experiences, particularly difficult ones.

How's the coffee or venue? Many venues are interesting or historic buildings, so your environment can be used to open conversations. Even brand chain hotels can be used as a conversation starter, as people can have such variable experiences of them. If all else fails, the quality of the food and drink on offer is always a pressing concern.

The people you are meeting will signal their level of enthusiasm for a longer conversation through their replies, their body language, and by whether or not they offer an open or closed response. Read the signs, and go with it, or move on.

Prompts and ideas

- Always remember a networker's job is to make conversation easy.
- Have some conversation starters that work for the context up your sleeve and ready for use.
- Listen to and observe the people you are meeting, and use what you see and hear to understand what they want to talk about. If they don't want to talk, move on politely.

Tip 35: Good questions

Make great conversations

One of the arts of great conversation is asking good questions. Some of these may be off the cuff responses to the discussion (you will get better at being spontaneous as your networking confidence grows). However, others can be prepared ahead, so long as you don't present them as, "and here's one I made earlier." Both kinds of questioning require practice, as well as a mindset that is about curiosity and interest rather than entertainment and ego. Paradoxically you will find spontaneous questions come to you more readily if you also have the security of some pre-prepared ones, because the act of preparing means that you have been thinking ahead, and you will find it easier to tune in.

Examples of questions you can flex and adapt to situations include:

Why did you come along to this event/group? Not, *Do you like these events?* because few people feel comfortable offering value judgements to a stranger. Never, *Do you come here often?* if you value your credibility.

What's been keeping you busy this week? is a bit more specific than the anodyne, *How's business?.*

What would you find really helpful from [the context]? You are aiming to create opportunities to become helpful with this question. Most importantly, you are setting the tone for a helpful and collaborative conversation.

Such questions often create openings to venture into more business-related topics you can expand on, for example:

How will [the budget] [the new guidance on] [the economic outlook] affect your [business] [clients] [customers]? The substance of the question will be informed by the context, but the basic structure is the same.

What do you see changing in your marketplace as a result of [what you've been listening to]? Or, a more generalised version for a less specific context: *What [has been] [do you see] changing in your marketplace [over the last year] [at present] [over the next 12 months]?*

What are your key priorities at present? This is a question to use after the conversation has developed for a while.

The first kind of questions are important in earning the right to advance to the next and more detailed question. Rapport is built gradually over the course of a conversation, as is the confidence to ask more complex questions and offer more detailed responses to the questions you are asked by others.

Prompts and ideas

- Prepare a few opening questions ahead of a networking opportunity. Even if you don't need them, having them available, and the thought you have put in will contribute to your confidence.
- Be prepared to ask simple questions first to get a conversation going: these earn you the right to advance.
- Listen intently and actively: listening informs you, and demonstrates that you value the other person's thoughts.

Tip 36: What you would discuss with friends …

Works for networking too

All too often in life the answer to a problem lies hidden in plain sight. When people say to me, "I don't know what to talk about when I meet someone new!" I ask, "What do you talk about with the people you already know?" Unless you have a very unique and narrow set of interests, the kinds of things you discuss with your friends are subjects that interest a wide range of people. Business doesn't exist in a vacuum; it is a vital part of society. Just by thinking for a few minutes about conversations you have recently had with friends, you will quickly spot subjects that are business-appropriate.

An obvious starting point is news stories. For example if there is a transport strike, there are social and economic consequences. With your friends you may discuss the challenge of getting to work, and in a business context you might ask if the disruption affects someone's business in particular ways. Many professionals have families, so news relating to education policy and student finance are a great example of things you would discuss at home, that business colleagues will also be concerned about, both from the personal point of view (in relation to their families), and the business point of view (being able to hire the right people).

In conversation with our friends, we often talk about things that could open up a whole range of business conversations. The price of fuel is a great example. This kind of conversational approach often creates good listening opportunities, particularly if you are able to frame questions about other people's businesses. Combining information with questions such as, "Our contacts are saying that situation X is having an impact on them. Are you finding the same in your market?" mark you out as someone who is both credible and interested. But remember, never breach client confidentiality in the hope of gaining a new contact.

Social interests are also fertile territory. My interests tend towards sport and outdoor activities, but for many others cultural interests and activities are equally useful. If you are near a town or city with a good arts centre or theatres, what (and often who) is on at the theatre may be interesting. Cultural information can be particularly useful when networking with people who are visiting from overseas, or who are new to an area.

Prompts and ideas

- Keep notes of subjects that recur in the office, at workshops and in conversation with your friends: these are the subjects that are exercising people at present, and will be as relevant to your new contacts as to your existing ones.
- Think beyond the business: news stories, cultural and social activity are all useful sources of ideas.
- Listen for opinions, different points of view and impacts that can provide a lead into other conversations, or a way of opening up a new topic.
- Challenge yourself every so often to note down your top five conversation subjects for the past day or week.

Tip 37: "Give to Get"

Be willing to give if you want to receive

I first came across the principle of *Give to Get* in a YouTube video from blogger and entrepreneur Seth Godin, and it is incredibly simple. If you want to receive something from someone then be prepared, willing and able to give something to them, or to do something for them. It is a fundamental truth masquerading as a statement of the obvious: so simple we forget it.

In networking, the *Give to Get* principle works in two ways. Firstly, if you want to get something back from someone in a conversation, you have to give something to that conversation. This doesn't have to be rocket science or even something they haven't heard before. So for example you might offer:

- A bit of background on your career.
- Reasons why you work where you do.
- What interests you or excites you about your work or your workplace.
- What you find helpful about the event you are at or the people you are working with.
- Sharing something you are interested in outside work.

The second way of thinking about *Give to Get* is as your prompt to ask questions at the end of your inputs (remember, good questions = great conversations). By putting in, you earn the right to receive back. *Give to Get* is the foundation of all good conversations, and by keeping it in mind, you will avoid monologues. *Give to Get* is as simple as asking, "And what's your opinion on ...?" or, "How's that impacting your business ...?" or, "Where does your interest in ... come from?" These questions help you build a dialogue, demonstrate interest and learn new information. There is no real downside for this one when networking.

For me, *Give to Get* is one of the cornerstones of good networking conversations because by giving information you are demonstrating your willingness to invest. By definition, a conversation is two-way and therefore you have to pass the focus and interest between each other in that conversation.

Prompts and ideas

- Be prepared to disclose information (business or social) about yourself if you want people to answer your questions.
- Ask questions at the end of your answers to pass the topic of discussion across and learn your contact's views.
- If you can't give something directly relevant, then offer what you do differently and why that is important to you.

Tip 38: Share your stories

Your narratives are your most effective tools

Let's define a story first of all (we're not talking *Once upon a time ...* here). A story in networking is an experience you have had and are prepared to share in order to build conversation. Your stories:

- Reveal something about you on a social or a work level.
- Provide a context for why you are present.
- Engage others in discussion by providing a personal experience or view.

To be a story of meaning or power, it must be interesting, memorable and engaging - an experience others can relate to. Early stage networking is not the time to tell someone you conquered the north face of the Eiger last summer, or you will seem boastful or scary (possibly both). When you offer stories that are a part of you, you are indicating a willingness to share something of yourself, making it easier for others to ask questions. Well told, concise, stories can easily open up ground for exploring areas of common interest and create the basis of a rapport on a business level, as well as on a social level.

We all find it easier to remember information given in stories because we make subconscious attachments to our existing memories. Stories make information easier to retrieve. Someone who reveals in conversation that they enjoyed a holiday destination you also really enjoyed will probably be easier to remember than the person who told you how many employees there were in their company.

Take the example of getting caught in the rain. Which are you most likely to remember, the person who tells you they got soaked this morning, or the person who tells you that they got splashed by a bus when they were trying to hail a taxi? Usually it is the person whose story gives you an image to associate with them and the event.

The final advantage of story sharing is that it invites others to share their stories too. If we disclose to others, they feel more confident and even subliminally obliged to share with us. All of this is part of rapport building.

Prompts and ideas

- Capture stories about your experiences that can be used when networking.
- Stories are not novels and definitely not fairytales, just experiences with you involved that provide some colour and make you memorable for positive reasons.
- Share stories to encourage others to remember you, engage in discussion, and share their stories too.

Tip 39: Listening builds trust

Are you listening to me or are you just rearming?

Listening is a skill, and one that requires a very conscious effort. The payoff for you is the power of listening in a conversation cannot be underestimated. Being properly listened to and heard is so rare that it is almost invariably flattering (in a positive way). For the listener, it adds to the value they gain from a conversation, and for the speaker it is rewarding and affirming.

Levels of listening

Disengaged: the lowest level of listening. Your body language and eye contact give away when you are not really interested, and when you have something else on your mind.

Hearing: this is what most of us do when we believe we are listening. Our ears are working, we hear the sounds, words and intonation but we are not paying sufficient attention to take in what the other person is saying.

Listening to reply: where you listen enough to be able to link what has been said to what you want to say. You are listening in order to find an opportunity to say what you want to say, believing this will create a connection. This usually comes across as us trying to be 'better' or more 'clever'. It will soon become clear that you are not fully engaging with or valuing the discussion. With practise, you can learn to catch yourself as you stop listening and begin to think about what you will say in reply.

Listening to understand: the highest level of listening, where you listen and value the information being offered. In doing so, and with the questions you ask, you demonstrate a wish or desire to know more. Your body language demonstrates your engagement, as you probe for more detail. Because you have been listening to understand, your curiosity doesn't come across as nosy or inappropriate.

When you listen to understand, you build the other person's viewpoint, perceptions and feeling for what it would be like to work with you. By building trust and properly engaging, you mark yourself out as someone who can deliver. People who listen build reputations for being great contacts to be around, people who really understand problems. Ultimately, people who listen are the ones you would call with a potential opportunity or challenge.

The lower levels of listening also generate a response, but it is not trust. New contacts are left under the impression that you might not listen when working with them. Would you listen to a brief, and would your own views be more important to you than theirs?

Prompts and ideas

- Learn to catch yourself if your attention drifts, and tune back into the conversation.
- Ask questions that grow out of what the other person is saying: challenge yourself to find out why people's experiences are different to yours, rather than telling them why yours are better or bigger.
- Keep listening: whilst it's important in networking, it's essential to relationship building.

Tip 40: Mirror, mirror

If someone wants to talk business, talk business: follow their lead

A primary aim of networking is to be seen as someone trustworthy, and for someone to trust you they must feel relaxed with you. Never underestimate the value of letting someone else set the agenda or pace. If you help the other person to feel comfortable, they are much more likely to trust you with information, be it professional or personal, in a conversation. The key to helping lies in paying attention and responding with emotional intelligence. The challenge is to remember to stop gabbling about yourself long enough to listen and observe.

- If your contact wants to talk mainly business then they will raise business-based topics or respond with more animation to business-based questions. Go with their choices. You can identify these by asking open questions such as, "What has kept you busy this week?" and noting whether the type of answer you receive is social or work-based.
- It is relatively simple to raise a social topic early on. For example, "How was your weekend?" or, "What plans do you have for holidays?" The depth of the answer you receive will give you a good indication as to the other's willingness to share personal information.
- Be mindful of how physically close someone wants to be during a discussion. What is the amount of personal space that makes them comfortable but not awkward with you? Be aware of whether they lean

into a conversation to show interest or whether they take a pace back to indicate a desire to observe and listen.

- Listen for clues about how they prefer to network going forward. Do they mainly work through meetings, email, social media, lunch or coffee? Such clues enable you to suggest a follow-up that fits with their preferences.
- Notice the length or conciseness of the answers you are given. If someone likes to elaborate, be prepared to mirror this in your own responses. Also, occasionally paraphrasing what they have said demonstrates you have listened. If the other person likes conversation brief and to the point, then keep it that way too. Short conversations are not necessarily bad conversations.

It is a sign of confidence to allow the conversation to develop in the direction your contact wishes. You will learn a lot, and make a good impression by doing so.

Prompts and ideas

- Spend more time listening and observing than talking. This will help you to notice what others want to talk about and how relaxed they want to be.
- Ask open questions so you can judge the quantity and quality of the responses you are given. This will allow you to adapt your approach to the contact.
- Great conversations feel comfortable and are reciprocal.

Tip 41: Your thoughts interest you

Now make them relevant to me

When you come across something that interests you it is easy to get on a bit of a roll. After all, you have stories and experiences to add, and you believe what you have to say is interesting and valuable. But there is a danger, or a risk for you here too. Once your interest is aroused, it is important to remember not to monopolise the conversation. If you do you will quickly become boring.

Have you ever been at a meeting or an event, or in a conversation and thought to yourself, "Okay that's enough now, please can I say something, or even better talk to someone else?" That is the impact you risk if you fail to involve the other person. You need to be aware of how you tailor what you are saying to the people you are meeting. There are three simple approaches:

- Support them: agree with what they are saying, or if you disagree, do it in a way that encourages conversation rather than shutting it down. Show interest through probing questions and support them in developing the conversation along their route.
- 'Bridge' to them: use your experience or story to make links with what your contacts are saying. Emphasise the similarities and shared interest or experience.
- Invite them: through your questions you can invite others to use your inputs as opportunities to ask for opinions and thoughts. Don't be afraid to give a view

or an opinion, but temper that by asking if the same is true for them or in their business.

The aim of these approaches is to ensure both of you are fully involved in the conversation, and that you are not trying to be the centre of attention. You need to modulate your approach for each individual. Some contacts will prefer you to make the pace of the conversation and *invite* them: this will help them to feel more comfortable. Others would prefer to be allowed to run the conversation and for you to *support* or *bridge*. By listening and observing the conversation, you can judge which strategy to use in each conversation or group.

Prompts and ideas
- Conversation can be made inclusive by endorsing what others say, building bridges between experiences, and leading with helpful questions.
- Tailor your approach to the people you are with. How much time do they seem to have to talk? Who's making the pace?
- Avoid dominating the discussion - hogging the conversation is the enemy of learning.

Tip 42: Venture into the unknown

If you stick with what you know, you will bore others and yourself

This is not a license to embroider your experience, or to make things up. It is a recognition that there are so many subjects that can come up in conversation, you simply can't prepare for them all. You will often be involved in conversations where you are not the subject expert, and your reaction to this can be telling, and not always helpful to your goals. If you decide *I don't know anything about that, I'd better keep quiet and stay out of this conversation.* Or, worse, *I don't know anything about this but I'm sure I can sound confident and convincing enough, I'll blag it,* you will miss valuable opportunities.

More positive thoughts, such as *I wonder what interests you about that?* Or, *I wonder if [someone I know or am working with] might be interested in that?* will also be communicated by your body language. There is an upside to not being the subject expert, and that is that it makes it much easier to listen. The downside risk is that by stepping back, literally or metaphorically, you may lower your impact and appear less interested.

It is important not to do what some confident (overconfident) networkers do, which is to appear engaged and contribute opinions despite a lack of knowledge. This might look strong, but potentially has two severely damaging impacts. Firstly, it can lead to you coming over as someone who believes they know something about everything, which is not an endearing characteristic. Secondly, if you are speaking to someone with deep expertise, you will quickly be found out. You will be asked a question the answer to which makes it clear your knowledge is weak or non-existent.

A questioning reaction, whilst seeming to be the obvious solution, can also be dangerous, because it is important not to let your lack of knowledge make you confrontational. Frowning, losing eye contact, a fading smile can all betray your emotions, and can create an impression of annoyance or disinterest. Avoid letting discomfort come over as disinterest.

View a new (to you) subject as an opportunity to learn new things and more about your new contact. Encourage them through listening. Don't be afraid to admit that this is not your area of expertise. Being honest and interested will gain you more respect than blagging. Affirming that the other person knows more than you both endorses them, and creates an opportunity for follow-up.

Prompts and ideas

- Be kind to yourself: you cannot possibly know everything, so prepare yourself to be interested as well as informative.
- Remain open to new ideas and information: networking is a learning opportunity, as well as a promotional one.
- Remember to keep your body language in check when you are on new territory.

ATTRACT

Creating attraction

A is for Attract, not, as I said before, attractive in the dating sense, but in the sense of being someone who others will find appealing to talk to, and potentially wish to work with. Everything I have talked about so far is about being professionally attractive. When networking, your professional attractiveness is manifest in the way you discuss things, ask questions, make suggestions or recommendations, display knowledge or expertise without appearing boastful, and by whether you are nice to be with.

To develop a business relationship, from the very outset each party to the relationship must find the other party(ies) sufficiently attractive to choose to engage. We can fill our time in many ways, but those who spend time networking widen the available choices about who they want to develop professional relationships with.

If you finish any conversation doubtful about whether you want to talk to that person again, or having made the decision you didn't enjoy their company, then it is unlikely you will choose to develop a relationship further, and of course this cuts both ways. People will be making the same judgements about you. As no one can possibly keep up with every new person they meet networking, we all go through a process of prioritisation or elimination at the end of each conversation: "Is this somebody I would like to spend time with again?" Therefore the close of any networking conversation must support the initial attraction.

The *Attract* stage of the GLAD Networking approach is about the last impression you will leave someone with at the end of a conversation. In their memory, it is probably their point of reference for the judgement they will make when they decide whether to pick up the phone when you call, whether to accept that meeting invitation, or whether they will attend the event you have suggested. So what thought are you going to leave them with? Will it be:

- That was awkward: we came to the end of the conversation and we didn't have anywhere to go with it.
- I will look forward to hearing more about [something you talked about], [he] [she] really seemed to want to help.
- I wasn't aware we could do something about that, I am looking forward to hearing [his] [her] ideas.
- [He] [she] clearly wasn't interested in me and wanted to talk to somebody else.
- It was good to meet someone who's also interested in [something you talked about]. I hope we can meet again and chat further.
- I wonder who else [he] [she] knows who can help me.
- I wonder how else [he] [she] could help me.

You have spent time trying to build your level of rapport,

engagement, interest and credibility throughout the conversation, so don't destroy it all by making a rushed or overly pushy impact at the end. Consider the behaviours you used during the greeting and the conversation: many of these still apply, along with a few others you can add to reinforce an attractive impact.

- Maintain your eye contact and remain focused on the person you are talking to. Looking round the room or making fleeting eye contact with others signals that you want to get away to talk to someone else.
- Keep listening and watching, and move at their pace.
- Mirror the close of conversation they want to have, thereby making it feel focused on them. Rushing the close gives the impression of being pushy. Taking longer than they want to will feel drawn out and possibly clingy.
- Paraphrase and summarise the things you have heard or learnt in the conversation. This both confirms your interest, and acts as a summary, indicating that the conversation is moving towards its end.
- A firm but simple handshake as you say a polite goodbye maintains the impression of someone confident.
- Smiling creates warmth, increases the impression of your having enjoyed their company, confirming attractiveness.
- Ask questions that demonstrate your commitment, even if it is as simple as, "Should I phone or email you to arrange that?" This creates a mutually agreed action, again confirming attraction.

The best end point for a networking conversation is a mutual close, with a follow-up action. When this happens, there is a sense that for both (or all) parties this is the best place to leave the conversation, and that it is to be continued. No one feels hurried, or pushed out of the conversation. If it is all about you, then your new contact will hear it in your language, observe your body language becoming focused elsewhere, and feel slighted by the speed with which you seek to close the conversation. You run the risk of wasting all of your hard work through their coming to the conclusion that you don't find them interesting, didn't have much to say, or you had seen someone more important to you. If you allow them to form this impression, not only will they not want to develop a business relationship with you, but you run the risk that they will relay their experience of you to others when given the opportunity.

Stages to achieve

Style of attraction

What style of attraction are you looking to achieve? If you have identified something of mutual interest that you can discuss, then you want a subject-specific or action-specific attraction. Alternatively, if your conversation was primarily based on establishing rapport, you are looking for a softer form of attraction: the wish to meet again and continue to explore business interests. These softer attractions are often by far the hardest in professional contexts, as the lack of a defined task focus or a follow-up mean that they are much more nuanced. You run the risk of your inner voice saying, "Why would they want to meet me again, what have I offered them?" and it is important not to fall into this trap. Just because a first conversation did not produce a clearly defined action, it doesn't mean that the door needs to be slammed shut.

Make it mutual

Closing a conversation where there is not an action-specific attraction in a way that is all about you doesn't work. It just comes over that you want to get away and have a conversation with somebody else. So think about how to create a softer attraction. Where possible use language that is about "we" or "us" or "you" rather than "I". For example, phrase proposals such as "Would it help you if ..." or "We could explore [something you have talked about] more over coffee ..." Avoid creating the impression that you are dumping someone unceremoniously in favour of someone potentially more rewarding to talk to.

Thanks and appreciation

Everyone responds to being appreciated, whether it is for their time, expertise, or their empathy. It also costs very little time or effort to let someone know we appreciate them, or something they have said. The hard bit is to remember to do it, or, for some people, to care enough to do it. "Thanks for your time, I really enjoyed talking with you about ..." is a great lead in to, "Perhaps we could meet up again and [explore that further] [discuss some other areas and ideas]."

Identifying next steps

People need to be attracted to something in order move further with it. In networking, moving forward is identifying the next step or follow-up action. So even with a softer style close, be clear about what you are proposing. You can do this by suggesting an action, who will initiate it, and a possible timeframe. In the spirit of a mutual action, seek their feedback and endorsement: "Would that be interesting to you?" or ,"How do you suggest we should action that?" As you gain experience, you will find suggestions that work for you. It is best if both (all) of you have responsibility for the next steps.

Obtaining contact details

This is so obvious, and yet somehow remarkably easy to omit. If there is to be a next step or action, then we need some contact details to follow up with. Traditionally contact details are provided in the form of business cards, but in some less formal contexts it is becoming increasingly common to be invited to connect on LinkedIn or in other social media and online groups. Sometimes people simply text each other at the end of a conversation to ensure that both parties know each other's contact details. The business card is far from dead, but it is no longer the only way to gather contact details, which is both an opportunity and a hazard. When business cards are not exchanged, you must ensure you have sufficient information about each other to maintain contact.

When it doesn't work

You have heard of failures of imagination? Often when I network, I see failures of attraction, and one of the main causes is the temptation to leap for a sale. Some people try to push the conversation to a close with a financially tangible and measurable result. In doing so, they generally end up with a contact who backs away defensively and rapidly. Networking is about opportunities to begin and to nurture relationships. If you are successful in this, and your goal is to develop new business, there will be plenty of time later, when a more trusting and credible relationship has been built. Looking for the short-term gain and pushing a sale quickly is not only pushy, but it is short-sighted and rarely results in long-term business relationships.

Again, our theme of making the *Attract* stage a mutual experience tells you that if you focus just on yourself, it is likely that there will be no attraction. Another hazard here is that many of the classic getaway lines are based purely on self: getting away, not making connection. It is obvious to the other person what you are doing, so if you choose these tactics, then be prepared to reap what you sow: a lack of connection.

Closes to avoid at all costs:
- I've just seen somebody I really need to talk to.
- I'm sorry but I need to leave now for an urgent appointment (and then not leaving).
- I need the toilet. (Just no. Too much information, and often untrue.)
- I've just finished my drink, I'll get another.
- I need to take this call. (A surprising number of people believe that this is acceptable, but it is not).

There is one final reason why learning how to close conversations at the same time as remaining attractive is an essential networking skill. If you don't learn to do it, you will only ever talk to one person per event you attend. This will be frustrating for you, and for those you talk to: they may feel coerced, or hemmed in by you (not attracted at all). Practising and refining your close is every bit as important as developing your greetings.

Tip 43: Try TLC

Thanks, link to future and contact details

You'll be familiar with the TLC acronym for 'tender loving care'. Networking also requires plenty of TLC: *thanks, links* and *contact*. When you are leaving a networking conversation, you want to show that it has been enjoyable or helpful, that you are interested in the other person, and that you want to build that relationship further. This is true whether you think you may have just found your next piece of business, or if you have only made contact and have no idea whether it will lead to something. In a relationship business (and networking is a relationship business) your actions and approaches need to build for the long term with TLC.

When leaving a networking conversation, TLC tells us the three areas to cover to achieve appreciation, empathy and connection:

T: make the other person feel that the conversation was worthwhile and you appreciated meeting them. You may have learnt new information, gained insight or simply widened the range of people you have access to. They have given you their time and attention and deserve your thanks. The opposite of making them feel appreciated, of course, is leaving them feeling unappreciated, which is not what you want to do. It really is as simple as saying, "Thank you".

L: link to future action – agreeing a future action creates momentum. It may be a catch-up email or call, a coffee, lunch, or even a meeting to discuss a specific issue or idea. Making this an action you are both involved in is the perfect reason for exchanging contact details.

C: exchange the necessary information to connect, either with a simple exchange of business cards, or digitally by sending each other a text message, or connecting on LinkedIn (or elsewhere). This is easier when you have already done the 'L' part. If you don't exchange business cards or telephone numbers, make sure you immediately note down as much as you know about the other person so you can find them on Twitter, Linked In, or however you have agreed to maintain contact.

Prompts and ideas

- Ensure the other person feels appreciated in a networking conversation, even when you are leaving on a soft close without an immediate piece of business to discuss.
- If possible, establish a link to future action, however simple: this invests you both in the relationship, and opens the door for asking for contact details through business cards or social media.
- Be prepared to connect in whatever way makes it easy for the other person. You want to make the connection, so make it simple.

Tip 44: If you value the contact

Take time to capture some details

When you are networking, you are working hard listening out for details and information in a conversation. People can transmit a lot of information in the course of a short conversation, and if you are listening attentively you can capture subjects to pick up on in a later call or email. There is nothing wrong with taking the time to record the information you have learnt. It should be specific to the individual, their interests, or their work and business. If you value building a relationship with the person, then this information is a critical link in developing that relationship, and you need to remember it.

There are many ways you can capture it: for example, you could write on the back of the business card you received from them. Some people I know make notes in a small notebook. Many people find a networking notebook helpful to remember the key points about new people they met. With a small enough book, it should be possible to make these notes discretely after the meeting, outside the event, or in a foyer at a conference. Increasingly I see people using their smartphones and tablets to do this, but do remember not to look distracted by your toys. If you don't like to write, leave yourself a voicemail on your business number: this not only records the details, but can act as a prompt to follow up the contact too.

Examples of the sort of information I record are:
- Business role and priorities

- Social interests and ways to relax (sport, hobbies and so on)
- Family information if shared, such as number, names and ages of children
- Reasons for attending
- Where we met.

Using good information in a follow-up action creates a positive impact. It demonstrates that you were listening, and are genuine in your interest, which contributes to the relationship-building space you are creating. It is not about how much you write or recall, but about capturing the key points to enable you to follow up on later. After each event, prioritise your follow-up actions, and ensure you make time for them.

If you value the contact you have just made, then a couple of minutes spent capturing key details is a worthwhile investment. The alternative is to forget, in which case, why did you have the conversation in the first place?

Prompts and ideas

- Listen carefully throughout the conversation for information about someone, including their interests and their work life, as well as the topics you can return to when following up.
- Capture the information you have learnt shortly afterwards. You can use the back of business cards you have gained, a small A5 size notepad, a notes feature on your phone, send yourself an email, or leave yourself a voicemail.
- Do something with the information you have learnt, otherwise the whole networking exercise is a bit pointless.

Tip 45: Only connect

Do not push to sell

Networking is the activity that connects you with other people in the hope of building relationships that will be helpful to both parties. Sales follow from building on our connections in a variety of ways. For example, creating a match between products, services and needs, or presenting a unique collection of benefits and selling points. In most cases, getting that far takes time.

Knowing the right moment to sell is the subject of many other books, but you will never get there if you don't build trust through developing rapport, empathy, and delivering reliably on the promises made in the early stages of contact, such as actually getting back to people by the date you suggest, remembering to send the link to an article you were talking about, and so on.

Matching needs with products and services requires time and understanding. There is nothing more damaging to your credibility than suggesting an incorrect solution or product. If you push your products or services too early, you risk alienating your contact. Faced with this, others push back with a defensive reaction, explaining why they have no need of that product or service. In a networking situation, they will usually quickly seek a different conversation to join.

Building trust with a business contact means you need to understand not just business requirements but also the individual, what's important to them and how they like to conduct business. All of these take time, patience and a willingness to understand before you start selling. It may also be that your services or products simply do not match their needs at this moment. Being honest about this can make for long-term relationships that pay back over time.

If you have had a great conversation and the opportunity is clear and understood, then offer your help, but put control of the discussion in the other person's hands. Your new contact may need time to reflect before acting on your suggestion.

Another great reason for parking the urge to sell, is that it will help you relax by removing a pressure. If you feel anxious to make sales, that anxiety will be transmitted in your body language. Selling and early-stage networking are two completely different activities. By regarding them as such, you enable your networking to be more productive, and you build more contacts to develop. In doing that, you maximise your downstream sales potential.

Prompts and ideas

- Measure your networking development by the number of connections you make that you can follow up and build a relationship with, not by sales made.
- Use your networking time to understand, learn and share.
- If you get lucky and meet someone who needs your services immediately, then offer to be helpful but be mindful that you have only just met.

Tip 46: A connection involves two people

Make offers of help to close

One of the easiest things to remember about a conversation is how it ended, particularly if you didn't like it. It is the most recent part of the conversation and so the easiest to recall. Phrasing the beginning of the end can often be a challenge for many of us. In workshops I am often asked, "How do I get away from someone if I've been with them for too long," or, "They're not the right person for me to network with," or even, "They're really boring." It is easy to forget that if the conversation feels like that to you, it almost certainly does to the other person.

A quick way would be to say, "Think we're done here, shall we move on?" or ,"I've run out of things to say, shall we exchange cards?" However neither of these phrases will leave a positive impact and memory.

I find, "Would it be helpful if … " a fantastic networking phrase. It is positive as it gives the control and decision-making power for the action to the other person. As a question, it involves both of us and provides the opportunity for a connection. Finally, it doesn't come over as too pushy or arrogant, so many of us will feel more comfortable using it as opposed to a more sales-driven phrase.

What you offer needs to be helpful and relevant to the conversation you have just had. Your offer should be informed by the level of listening you have put into the conversation. You may well have had a productive discussion covering an opportunity, challenge or problem, in which case you can build your close around that. For example, "Would it be helpful if I summarised our discussion in an email for you and included a couple of case studies I know of?" This creates the reason to ask for contact details so you can do this.

I have seen some terrible closes, such as *I need the toilet/ a drink/a cigarette*, followed by the same person walking up to someone new to have a fresh conversation (as if the person left behind won't notice). Another disaster I have been on the receiving end of: *I've just seen XX and I am desperate to see him* ... I wanted to say, "By all means, don't let me waste your time any longer," (but didn't, of course).

Not all conversations offer immediate opportunities, so sometimes it is about closing off the conversation. "It's been great to meet you, would it be helpful if we exchanged contact details and perhaps I could call you when I'm around your area?" You are still making an offer and leaving the decision and sense of control to your new contact. Even if the answer to the *Would it be helpful ...?* questions was no, there is an opportunity to check with your contact what would be helpful. This way you may still create a mutual action you are committed to.

Prompts and ideas

- "Would it be helpful if ... ?" makes an offer to your new contact in a manner that leaves the control shared between you.
- Try to avoid old techniques to break off conversations. Everyone's been on the training course and knows what you're doing.
- Be genuine about ending a conversation: if you want to move on and network more, then say so politely. Try to exchange details and move on.

Tip 47: If not now?

Do not dismiss a new connection if there is not an instant payback

A constant networking challenge is avoiding the tendency to be impatient when you don't see an obvious or immediate return on your efforts. It is easy to begin to feel the pressure, and want to move on to talk with someone else. Such short-termism, ignores the fundamental principles of networking:

- Networking is about building relationships not making immediate sales.
- Networking is a long-term activity not a short-term gain.
- Networking is about other people, not you.

Whilst someone may not be offering an immediate return on your conversation, or a sales opportunity to follow up on, there are numerous other ways they could be valuable to your network. For example, they may provide a gateway into their own network, which might contain many contacts you would like to meet. They may not be a buyer of your services now, but how long will it be before they are, and who will they mention you to before then? They could be someone with several years' experience in your industry, presenting you with an opportunity to learn, gain new perspectives and access new ideas.

Even if you are right and this connection is not able to help you in some way, or you cannot help them, what if they can help a colleague, a friend or a client? Just because there is no obvious or immediate payback, it does not follow that they are not interesting. You can significantly enhance your reputation by linking people together in your network when they need help. The networking outcome is not always about a sale for you, it may be for someone else who then feels a stronger relationship with you because of your help.

Be open to what someone's value could be beyond the current conversation. Seek to build conversations that will lead to relationships that can identify and reveal value.

Prompts and ideas
- Treat all connections as valuable when finishing conversations as you never know when they will be, and networking is about the long term.
- Focusing on the conversation and identifying relevant interests is the best way to leave a conversation, and enhances your reputation.
- Connections can be helpful to you and to your colleagues, clients and friends. The value doesn't always come to you; passing it to others enhances your reputation and relationships.

Tip 48: Contact details

Tools to make it easier, sometimes make it harder

We established earlier that you need to offer *Thanks, Links* and *Contact* (TLC). In order to maintain contact, you must establish how. If you can't be efficient about agreeing on this, it suggests you are inefficient or ineffective. Or worse, it looks like you are making excuses and in fact you are not really interested. The fact that not everyone carries business cards (personally I do, and see no reason to stop), makes things more difficult than they were when I started off in business.

To my mind, all of the following statements about cards all sound like excuses:

- *My cards are being updated and are at the printers.* You could have planned an overlap of cards in this situation. You are just flagging up poor planning and preparation.
- *I'm sorry I don't have my cards on me, I've left them on my desk.* This tells me that you don't think about your networking before leaving and so networking wasn't a priority.
- *I don't do business cards, they are a bit old-fashioned and I only end up throwing them away.* Focus on what you do do (LinkedIn, Twitter), and don't insult the person who has just offered you their card by saying they are old-fashioned.
- *My cards aren't very impressive so I'm having them redesigned. I think it's important your cards say the right thing about you.* When I heard this the first time my

inner voice said, "My card says I'm ready to network and serious about business; your lack of a card says you're not." But I smiled, and remained polite.

If you aren't offering cards, you must have an alternative. Offer to exchange mobile numbers, or make sure the other person knows how to find you on LinkedIn or elsewhere. The advantage with social networking sites is that the connection can be made immediately. Sometimes this can even lead to a new conversation, "How do you use [LinkedIn] [Twitter] [Facebook] [Instagram] in your business?" I never bank on there being internet connection, or phone signal at all venues. I may not always need cards any more, but unlike the internet, cards never 'go down'. If you can remember your details you could offer to write them on your new contact's card, an agenda for the event or a publicity leaflet (giving them more chance of remembering where they met you). This at least gives the impression of someone who finds solutions to problems, and is genuinely interested in connecting.

Prompts and ideas

- Plan your business cards, particularly when you are having them reprinted, to ensure you always have some available. Have a contingency card printed to cover your networking while you are waiting.
- Ensure your social networking profile provides more than business card information, so that people can learn more about you.
- Don't make excuses: find ways to offer a connection. Somebody once said to me, "Bring me a solution not a problem." Try to do that for yourself as well as others.

Tip 49: Social media matters

Manage your profiles

I review a lot of social media profiles as part of my networking workshops, providing feedback and discussing the ways people can make their profile more helpful and attractive. The key question is, what does the reader want from a great profile? After all, you loaded it up to help others meet you, know more about you, and become interested in what you offer.

Many profiles I see fall into the 'because I had to' category. Profiles of people who were pestered into it by colleagues. They put a page up with minimal detail, but really shouldn't have bothered. A profile without good information is worse than no profile at all, as it marks you out as someone who does't care.

Other profiles I see just put up a listing, not quite a CV as that would 'sell' what the individual has done at each job, and show why it was interesting. Listings are just that: a litany of positions held, possibly with some experience gained, or key skills; but without description or specifics.

What you want from your profile, and how much you want others to see will vary depending on the conventions of your industry or sector, the stage you have reached in your career, the journey you took to get there, and how much of what you have done it is possible or appropriate to share. So look around your network at other profiles: look for what you think works, for approaches you like and the kind of information being shared. Learn from what others do well, as well as from what they do badly.

Consider ways you can make your profile personal and memorable. Decide what kind of photo to use (formal and professional is usually best, although in the creative industries I have seen some wonderful and very recognisable avatars). The images you put up help other people to recognise you, and show things about you. The visuals you use and the text you post should all work towards helping you meet your social media and networking goals. You may be looking to build a reputation in an area, increase your profile in an industry, or simply advertise your skills. Whatever your focus is, use appropriate, 'internet-searchable' terms consistently, and create repetition to assist viewers' memory.

Always review what you have written from the point of view of a reader, your audience. It is they who count.

Prompts and ideas

- Review the profile pages you like, what makes you want to read them, and is that the impact you want yours to create?
- Read your current profiles and honestly write down the value you think a new contact could take from your page.
- Ensure your social networking profile provides more than a business card, so that people can learn more about you.

DEVELOP

Begin to build the relationship

The final stage of GLAD networking concentrates on what happens after the first networking conversation, which can vary widely: from feverish activity to help resolve an issue; to complete silence. The actions you choose will have an effect on your ability and confidence to take the relationship forward. The aim of networking is to provide opportunities to build relationships, not to have endless one-off conversations, so it is critical that you spend time on effective next steps. There are four main ways to proceed: proactively, reactively, passively, or dismissively.

Proactively

By taking the initiative, prioritising your follow-up actions, and creating possibilities for further interactions through which a relationship can be built, proactivity confirms your desire to build the relationship and your interest in the contact, thereby increasing your chances of success. A proactive follow up maximises the usefulness of the opportunity and the information you gained.

Reactively

By relying on an external stimulus, your response may still be prompt, once the stimulus has been received, be it an email from them, or a reminder actioned. While not taking the lead in proactively developing the relationship, this response can still work, particularly if it has been agreed that the other person will take primary responsibility. However you are dependent upon the other person following up effectively.

Passively

A passive response is driven by the other contact, without initiation or encouragement from you, and often indicates to the other party that you are not genuinely interested, or have too many other priorities to make an effort. The impact of this on your new contact is to show your disinterest, giving the impression the other party is not a priority and their future business is not needed.

Dismissively

A dismissive approach is one in which you elect not to engage further in the relationship, either due to prioritising other tasks as more important, or because you have decided that this relationship is not of value to you. Some people might say that they simply forgot, under pressure of work, but so far as I am concerned, forgetting is the same as dismissing. A dismissive response is likely to be mutual and low-impact, but it does carry risk to your reputation. Moreover if, in changed circumstances such as a change of job, company or role, you ever need to pick up on the contact, it will be extremely hard to do so.

The further down this list of ways of proceeding you are, the more likely it is that you will have wasted your time. I can never understand why people invest so much time meeting new contacts, having interesting discussions, and exchanging details, never to follow up on them.

Focus on being proactive

How long does it take you to forget someone's name or any details about them after you have met them: weeks, days, or even minutes? Someone once confided to me that he would often begin to lose details and names in the time it took him to get to the elevator (probably because he hadn't actually been listening in the first place). But in a world where smartphones deliver constant demands on our immediate attention, via email, SMS and calls, it is very easy to let this happen.

The tips in this section are designed to help you to be proactive in your follow-up. They will not only help you to make a better return on your investment of networking time, but will also ensure you are remembered by other people for the right reasons. Each interaction you create as part of the *Develop* stage of the process begins the networking cycle again. In follow-up conversations the *Greet* stage can be shorter: move quickly into *Learn, Attract* and *Develop*. Your positive networking attitude should be fuelled and improved by the successes you achieve in developing relationships, and will provide material for your future networking. Keep returning to your networking strategy to ensure the actions you take with your contacts at the *Develop* stage are both helpful *and* are meeting your goals. Finally, you will be building your impact still further with each contact, each email, phone call, and each meeting. Building on your impact is a relationship-long activity.

What stops *Develop* from happening?

It is common sense to follow up on contacts, and yet in my experience from workshops and in coaching others, this is the area where many people end up feeling frustrated and annoyed by their lack of results from networking. They have met a lot of new people, established contacts and swapped details, but they have not taken those contacts on to the next step. The realities of their busy work and social lives mean that following up on networking remains at the bottom of their priority list, with the knock-on impact that the time they have invested so far has effectively been wasted.

After a meeting, you often return to the office and progress the immediate action points from the meeting. You may even debrief with other colleagues who were at the meeting, or who are involved in other business with this client. As we established much earlier in this book, you will often meet new people in the course of ongoing projects. If you have maintained your networking attitude, then the actions relating to firming up on new contacts made at the meeting will be included in your debriefing discussions. If you haven't, they will be lost in the urgency of meeting other deadlines.

A further problem people mention is not knowing what to follow up on. I often hear, "What should I call or email them about? I can't just say, 'How's business?'" To which I am often very tempted to reply, "Why not?" At least that would demonstrate an interest, unlike complete silence. But if you have applied the tips and ideas in the *Learn* section of this book, you know how to establish a range of shared subjects and interests to talk to them about. You will have listened to people and therefore you know what they would find interesting in a call. You may even have researched some helpful information or identified a useful colleague to introduce them to. The key barriers seem to be:

Existing work being the priority: this will always be the case assuming you are successful. To remain successful in the long term you will need a healthy network, and so prioritising this is key to your future business. Priorities are about choices, and in the end it is down to us to choose.

*Lack of time: a*lmost all of us complain we don't have enough time, but how we use our time is our choice. We are not the passive victims of the clock. Find time; make time. Email from the train on the way home; say no to another task; set aside time. If you make the effort, you can achieve a great deal in a remarkably short time. Follow-up is the easy bit: all the hard work has already been done.

I don't know what to say: this is not an adequate excuse, because there are many ways to follow up, and if you were listening properly, you have gathered points and information to pick up on.

My overall message here is that following up in the *Develop* stage is a choice. Plenty of things can prevent you from following up, but every reason not to follow up is outweighed by reasons why you should be making the effort:

- Future business
- Building a profile
- New job opportunities
- Personal interest and social enjoyment
- Learning and knowledge-building.

Your options are to make time to *Develop* or to make a choice not to, and dismiss it.

Easy steps

So, what are the easy things you can do? Here are six simple rules to help focus on developing your new contacts into relationships.

Listen

It is a lot easier to follow up with someone if you have spent sufficient time and attention listening to them in your conversation. Use the tips in the *Learn* section of this book and they will show you the threads to follow up with people, the areas of common interest you have, the questions or concerns they have, or the information you shared with each other.

Capture

Capture the information you heard. You don't need everything but a couple of thoughts, ideas and topic areas captured in a networking notebook, or on the back of a business card, will provide prompts for future conversations. They can also be helpful when keeping an eye out for interesting articles, news stories and publications. It is an impressive lead in to a follow-up call or meeting when you can say, "I was reading this and it made me think of you and our conversation." This says *I was listening, I remembered and I'm thinking about you.* All good attributes if someone is looking for a professional to work with.

Prioritise

As we have identified, the most common killer of developing relationships by networking follow-up is failure to prioritise. After you have had a networking conversation or opportunity, think about the actions you can prioritise immediately afterwards. What do you need to do urgently, and what can be done in the next week? Also, schedule some reflection time on a monthly basis to consider how you are following up your contacts. Who have you seen recently? Which relationships have you progressed? Who are you in danger of ignoring?

Small things count

It is not just the big things that get us remembered. Often people recall those who have been around consistently over a longer period of time, providing helpful information, keeping up to date and showing an interest. So if you don't have something big to share, are you able to meet up because you are visiting another client or customer nearby? Have you sent an email recently, or made a call to see how business is going and if any new challenges or opportunities have arisen for your client or customer?

Monitor

Keep an eye on how you are doing, and be honest with

yourself. Sometimes we neglect our network; it is not terminal, and we can always recover this with a little time invested. It is important you understand what you are doing and why. You can use the goals you have set yourself in your networking strategy to help determine what you should be monitoring. For example, is your success measured by volume of contacts, number of meetings, and new business opportunities created; or is it through access to new expertise, opportunities to speak at events, and career opportunities offered? One way to monitor and measure is through using a task management system (such as on many email calendars); others use a simple spreadsheet; and many use social platforms such as LinkedIn to provide prompts to action.

Feedback

Look for feedback on how you are doing. Do you approach your contacts in a way that works for them, with an appropriate frequency, with the right information and using the right channels (online or face to face)? Seeking feedback is a brave move for many people, but it shows a real sense of caring and wanting to develop a relationship that works for both parties.

Whatever you do in the *Develop* stage of your networking, do something. If you do nothing, be prepared to be forgotten, to potentially be ignored when you could have been helpful, and to have spent a lot of wasted time networking with new individuals. As Dr Pepper likes to say, "What's the worst that can happen?" At worst, your contact may say "Not today thanks." They are highly unlikely to say, "Why are you contacting me, go away and don't come back!"

Tip 50: Follow up contacts quickly

Even if just to say, "Hello, great to meet you, can we catch up again?" Help them remember you

Unfortunately for all of us, it can take a very short time to forget somebody after you have met them. We have several demands on our time, through work or social life, and our brains have to remember a large amount of short-term details. If you are a new contact for someone, your name is, at best, part of their short-term memory, and is liable to be forgotten as other details become prioritised in front of it.

Therefore the importance of follow-up is to:

1. Help the other person remember you.
2. Link your name to something in their long-term memory, or to a subject they will retain, for example a business issue, or a common interest.
3. Signal the importance of the new contact to you.
4. Demonstrate your desire to build a professional relationship with them.

Even if you don't have a specific action such as a meeting to arrange with them, or a publication to suggest to them, then a short call or email to say: "It was great to meet you and I hope we can stay in touch," can help this process. You can enhance this by adding in some of the subjects you discussed when meeting. For example:

- *When you start work on that issue, I'd be happy to meet and have a coffee to discuss it and offer our experience.*
- *Once the [football], [rugby], [cricket] season has got going*

perhaps we could have lunch or a drink to compare the success or otherwise of our teams.

Such links help provide a stronger connection in your memory for recognising, remembering, and thinking of your contacts.

If you don't follow up, the challenge has to be, "Why did you network in the first place?"

Prompts and ideas

- If you are investing an hour in networking and meeting new people, it must be worth ten minutes to follow up with an email or a phone call.
- Link the conversation you had with the follow-up you are making. This will demonstrate listening, and links your name to other details in their memory.
- Avoid procrastinating because you don't think your follow-up is good enough: just do it!

Tip 51: Avoid procrastination

There can always be reasons not to follow up, so keep your actions simple and immediate

When faced with following up your networking, you can easily get caught up in procrastination, and leave it to a point where it feels too difficult or too much of a surprise to the new contact. You might then rationalise your-self into not doing it at all. Some people's work lives and personal lives are so busy that the follow up of new con-tacts simply never reaches the top of the 'things to do' list.

If you keep the actions simple and immediate, you reduce both of these problems. By keeping them simple, you reduce the length of time or effort involved. The passage of time is a key trigger for procrastination, which then leads you to rationalise the follow-up as lower priority. By acting promptly, your follow-up is more genuine, there is less memory recall required on the part of your new contact, and you don't permit the passage of time to make this task a bigger deal than it actually is.

Here are some simple examples of phone calls, emails or actions you can do the next day, or later the same day:
- Ask for feedback on how the meeting, event or presentation went.
- Check to see if there are other events, publications, or colleagues they would find interesting, (you will have gained some sense of this from your initial meeting and from your questions).
- Send a recent news story or blog that you think they

will find interesting based on the context or subject
matter of the meeting or event.

- Arrange a future meeting to discuss a particular
  opportunity or issue in more depth or to introduce
  an expert colleague to the discussion.
- Connect on social media platforms such as LinkedIn.
  If you mention the location or context in which you
  met them, they are more likely to remember you.
- Add the contact to relevant publication lists or
  distribution lists from your firm or company. Be
  careful to ensure these are tailored or personal when
  distributed or they will be treated as spam.

Prompts and ideas

- Keep the follow-up action simple to ensure you do something, and you do it
  quickly.
- Use the subject matter of your conversation to keep the follow-up relevant,
  even if it is just to refer to the social element of the conversation in a quick,
  'good to meet you' style email.
- Consider how you could follow up face to face, verbally or online. Use the
  approach most comfortable for your new contact: you want to be
  remembered positively.

Tip 52: Keep your follow up promises

If you forget to do the easy things, then they won't remember you for the hard ones

We all tend to make a lot of promises about when we will call people, information we will send them, emails of dates we could meet or have coffee, and so on. How many of these promises do you keep and how long does it take you to act on them? Such promises are easy to make and relatively easy to deliver on. An email with some information attached, or some availability in your diary doesn't take long to write. The disadvantage is that for this very reason, you might leave it, your inner voice saying, "You can do that any time, focus on this urgent stuff now." Then you might leave the task until it has been uncomfortably long since you made the promise. Or, even worse, you just don't do it at all.

Your delivery on promises is part of your initial impact on a new contact. They have met you, taken some messages and made some judgements from the way you look, sound, and the subjects you talked about or showed interest in. Now they will see how you perform when delivering on the things you have said. If you fail to deliver, or you take a long time doing so, what impression will they take away? I suspect it will be something like: "Well if it takes that long to send me a publication or some dates, I wonder how quickly they can respond to a difficult or pressurised query?" Or: "He/she clearly is not that bothered, I'll find someone who wants to work with me."

It is tempting to make a promise to end a conversation and get away from someone, and it may be the right thing to do, but a note of caution: don't make false promises. You may not intend to build a relationship with this person but they will be able to talk about you to others: "Yes, they promised to get back to me too, so I wouldn't hold your breath waiting for them." Your promises and your delivery on them are a key part of your integrity, and will build or destroy your reputation, so don't damage yourself by neglecting simple follow-up tasks.

Keep a list of the promises you have made whilst networking, summarise any at the end of a conversation, and add them to your list. Ensure you address your list quickly, even if it is by email to acknowledge the promise or action you committed to. This will tell your new contact you are serious, and will begin to build your reliability and ultimately your trustworthiness with them.

Prompts and ideas

- Note down the promises you make after each networking conversation, ensuring these are added to your things to do list and prioritised.
- Don't leave it longer than four days to send any emails or phone calls you have promised. If needed, send a holding email to confirm any actions you are taking that will take a while to complete.
- Don't make a false promise in order to get rid of someone. You will create a negative impact, and potentially damage your personal reputation.

Tip 53: I'm going to be in your area ...

Make an offer of networking, without the pressure of a sell

Calling someone to ask for a meeting can be a pressurised task. Pressure for you because you are hoping they will say yes, and you feel the need to offer a reason for the meeting: something of value the other person will want to take. Pressure for them, because they are put on the spot to say yes, find an excuse to not meet, or provide a blunt no.

One of the best ways I have found of achieving follow-up meetings is to offer times when you will be in their area or city anyway. Firstly, there is a reason for the trip anyway (another business meeting, a new introduction, a client piece of work), which reduces the risk for you that the trip will become a wasted one. Secondly, your contact gets the message that you already work in their area, which would make future contact and work easy to organise. Finally, if your contact knows you have something else on, they are under less pressure to agree or to offer an excuse not to meet.

I have several contacts who say, "Just call me on the day and see if I'm free, that way I won't feel I have to call and cancel if something comes up." There are others who want to arrange the meeting in advance and will stick to that arrangement. It always helps to know what type of follow-up will work best for your new contact. Asking at the *Attract* stage demonstrates your awareness of this and your desire to make it easy for them to stay in touch and work with you.

Your diary is already likely to be full of opportunities to build on networking contacts, by reconnecting when you are in a person's area, but too often you see just the tasks and the work, and forget to look for the opportunities. For example, where will you be tomorrow and who does that give you a chance to meet? It doesn't have to be an external contact or even mean leaving the office. Have a look around you: who haven't you spoken to for a while; who is new in the office; who do you need to get to know better in your network? Ask them if they fancy a coffee or sharing lunch later: take the opportunity to know more about them.

Prompts and ideas

- Look for opportunities in your diary: where will you be that gives you the opportunity to follow up with new contacts? Before starting your business meetings, could you catch someone over a coffee to see how they are and how business is going?
- Email or phone to arrange follow-ups in their area. If you suspect they are going to be busy, a short email is easier to reply to and also doesn't put your contact under pressure.
- Is there someone in your office you haven't met? Ask them for a coffee during the day, and share some information about what you both do.

Tip 54: What will I invest to build a relationship here?

Be honest and act on the relationships you want to build

The level of investment you make in contacts after meeting them depends on the goals and potential areas of value for each party in the relationship. With limited time available, you should make informed choices about the relationships you choose to invest in and develop further.

For example, with new business opportunities look at contacts in this area, and plan based on the answer to a number of key questions:

- What does this contact want, and am I well placed to deliver it?
- How well does the contact know me: are they only just becoming aware of me or is there a previous contact or experience?
- What will it take to be considered as a sensible choice of adviser or supplier to this client?

Decide on the length of time you want to invest in the relationship, and also the activity you will need to undertake. Your aim is to be in your contact's thoughts for the right opportunities.

Alternatively, a reputation-building opportunity gives you the chance to increase your profile in a given area of expertise or industry, so the choice of who to invest in should assess whether that contact will increase your profile. Maybe they can introduce you to members of their network, or are prominent in a relevant industry or networking group. Perhaps they write for publications with a helpful readership.

For a contact to be a learning opportunity for you, they need to be at a higher level of expertise than you, or have an ability to identify new thinking and possibilities. With learning-based contacts, simply keeping in touch through social media platforms, reading and commenting on blogs, or exchanging ideas will be sufficient.

No contacts should be discarded completely, as you never know when they will become valuable. I call them the 'unknown opportunities'. It can be tempting to say, "This person doesn't need me," or "This person isn't interesting," but to do so is short-sighted. Consider what action or investments you are prepared to make in your unknown opportunities. For example, sharing information or insights with them via social media, inviting them to events, or, posting publications that are relevant.

Prompts and ideas

- Categorise the contacts you meet into those who you are prepared to invest in now, those who are medium term, and those who are long term.
- Consider your plan of action based on the networking goals you have for each relationship.
- Don't discard contacts. You are targeting your levels of effort to ensure the right, appropriate and best return on networking. Seek to hold onto all your contacts, as they may be valuable fairly soon.

Tip 55: Network in your clients' businesses

Ask who else can I meet? Can you introduce me to them?

At a client site on a project or any piece of work, you have opportunities to ask your client contact to introduce you to others. This allows you to widen your network and create the impact of being interested, wanting to broaden your knowledge, and to become part of their business in a more active and involved way.

Often when working, you may stop at the task you have to complete, and fail to look for the learning possibilities, or the opportunities to develop further. It is also possible your client contact hasn't considered introducing you to others until you actually ask. By prompting their thinking, you establish new links, or at a minimum leave them with an impression of wanting to help and be involved.

You want to appear adequately prepared to your client, so consider in advance the areas where you think you could add more value. That is to say, think it through before starting the conversation. Choose an appropriate time to ask (often a closing question in the conversation, or a response to a specific opportunity or issue). Be careful not to use the request as a conversation driver when it could look pushy or inappropriate. Finally, have the courage to ask your contact, "Would it help to meet another person in the business?" or "Is there anyone else you think I/we should be talking to in your organisation or network?"

In line with my other tips you also need to act proactively

on the information you are given. While it is great to ask and get a new contact name, that will not develop the relationship on its own. Acting on the new lead will start that process and provide the connection. So follow up quickly or, as in all networking, run the risk of damaging your reputation and starting again from the beginning with that contact.

Prompts and ideas

- Prepare for the networking element of a conversation that may identify opportunities to speak with others in your client's business.
- Have the courage to ask people who else they know who you could connect with to discuss common interests or ideas.
- Follow up on people you have been referred to: people who talk to each other regularly will probably mention the conversations in which they referenced each other, and an expectation has been created.

TO SUM IT ALL UP

CONCLUSION

Be authentic and be proactive with it

I have been through lots of tips and ideas that have helped me, my colleagues and friends over the course of our networking careers. There are all sorts of opportunities to get to know people, share information and become part of their network: more than when my career started.

The growth of networking venues and opportunities arises from the increasing mobility of the professional population, the growing number of tools and apps to help us, and the importance of networks in all aspects of our lives. There are also many more ways for people to get to know us, to observe how we behave and to hear and read the things we say and share with others. People have access to all sorts of information that helps them reach conclusions about who we are and how authentic we are.

The role of trust in personal and business relationships has always been important, and the increase in networking opportunities also equals an increase in competition for attention. Simply being the most vocal, the most visual, the most entertaining, the cleverest or even the best at what you do is not enough. What matters above all else is authenticity.

The opportunities we have as professionals, new business owners, academics and even as undergraduates are about how much we choose to engage and be proactive about networking with others in order to build our profiles. Opportunities are there for us to take. The questions are whether we want to take them, and if so, how do we go about doing so?

To be certain that we build, maintain and grow the network that we want to have in order to achieve our business and personal goals, we must be proactive and take charge of the networking we do.

So to conclude, here are ten things you can do in the next few weeks to get started.

Set your goals

Set yourself clear and measurable goals for your networking. Start with an initial aim, describing what you want to achieve as a result of your networking. This will set a context for your networking and give you focus in the decisions you make. For example, your aim may be about being an expert or 'go to' person in a given industry or discipline. Rather than just writing in management speak, define what becoming an expert in your area would require in terms of actions, behaviour and outcomes. Ask yourself, "How will I know I have achieved this goal?" and then use the answers to that question to set some measurable targets.

The more measurable you make your goals, the more

focused your objectives will be and the more effective your evaluation of the success or need for changes in your networking strategy. To reach your goals, set some objectives. Do not overdo it though: around three to five objectives are likely to suffice. Objectives should be more specific than your goals and, to borrow a regularly used phrase, they should be SMART (Specific, Measureable, Aspiring, Realistic and Timely). Examples of your objectives might include:

- Joining a relevant industry body within three months and attending at least three events over the next year.
- Reconnecting with alumni colleagues by
  - attending the firm's alumni programme events this year, or
  - contacting two people per month and arranging a follow-up coffee or lunch.
- Reconnecting with a minimum of 10 people over the coming year.
- Publishing an article via a blog, industry publication or corporate newsletter regarding your area of expertise, demonstrating your experience and point of view on the issues involved. (Always set yourself a deadline for this kind of objective.)

To test your goals and objectives, share them with a colleague or mentor. Seek feedback not only on the goals but also the objectives and ideas you have for achieving them. Making your goals and objectives public or at least semi-public in this way will increase the accountability you feel for achieving them, and also make great use of the experience and ideas around you.

Make it about you

In every aspect of your networking, make your actions about *you* as an authentic networker. Aim to network in situations and environments that suit your strengths and make you feel comfortable enough to be true to your character and the things that make you who you are.

Be honest enough with yourself to recognise which networking environments you thrive in, and which you find challenging. This is not to say you should ignore the ones where you have a weakness, but start with the ones where you are confident, and practise your skills. With the confidence you gain, you can then gradually expand that authenticity into the environments you find more challenging.

A hearty dose of self-awareness about what is important to you in networking relationships, the approaches you take to business and clients, and about your strengths and weaknesses will help. Take some time to reflect: where have you been successful in networking in the past and how? Evaluate what it is people enjoy about working with you. You may even seek some proactive feedback from existing and new clients. Remember, all feedback is a gift. When you receive a great present, one given with care and feeling, you enjoy using it in your life. If it is given without that care, or is an unhelpful present, then you can either throw it away or leave it in the attic!

Get your online game together

Online networking and social media platforms are part of what is happening in networking today. Your choice is very simple: be part of online culture in a meaningful way that helps to build a profile, or choose to opt out and accept that there are conversations or activities that begin online which you will not be part of or invited to.

Audit and evaluate your existing social media presence by asking some simple key questions:

- Which platforms are you on and what purpose is that meeting for you?
- When you look at your profile what would make you want to contact this person, what would make you not want to, and what is missing completely?
- How much time will you invest to make your efforts consistent?
- Which groups of people are gathering on the platforms you are involved in, and should you be participating more (or less)?

Remember, as with face-to-face networking, inconsistent online networking looks insincere.

Then make a list of simple steps you can take to put the right information out there about you and to ensure people are reading the right messages about you.

- Does your profile on each platform have a photo and is that photo appropriate to the people viewing you there?
- Have you updated your experience, job roles and skills?
- Who do you already know on that platform?
- Have you searched current and ex-colleagues, existing clients, or clients you have worked with in the past?

- Are you connected with all your friends in other professional sectors?
- Is your profile SEO friendly?
  - Have you used key words on a regular basis?
  - Have you kept the titles easily understandable and linked to the value or work you provide?
- Are you participating fully in the culture of giving and receiving recommendations and endorsements?

Evaluate your existing network

Everybody has an existing network based on the experiences they have had to date. Your network has been established through everything you have done to date. As with your online audit, evaluating the breadth and health of your current network will enable you to decide on the areas where you want to improve. You will also find the process of evaluation will boost your confidence: you have already established numerous relationships.

Review two aspects of your existing network: *quality* and *quantity* of relationships. Quantity is easy to measure. Determining the quality of each relationship will require more thought, but it will help you to identify which of them will be most useful to you in the process of further expanding your network.

To evaluate your existing network, it helps to list your relationships in categories, for example by industry area, by client company, organisation, or by areas of expertise and knowledge. Categorising your contacts in this way enables you to focus on the areas you have already built networks in, and the areas you wish to expand into. Once you have that list, you can begin to identify who is missing, whether it is organisations, job titles, roles or even names.

The people you already know may be your bridge and link to being introduced to the people you need to know. It is a lot easier to ask someone you know for an introduction when you have done a bit of research about who it is you would like to be introduced to and why.

Remember, as anyone in networking will tell you, quantity of contacts is nice but is not the ultimate purpose or goal. The quality of the quantity will come from whether you are building networks in the right places, with people who want to build further.

Therefore the quality is key and you can develop your own metrics for assessing the quality of each individual in your network. One metric is who can they introduce me to, another is whether they are empowered to engage professional services such as the ones you offer.

Traffic light systems (green for great relationship, amber for in need of development and red for not off the ground yet) can also be helpful in understanding the level of relationships and the further development they need. From this exercise you can identify the action areas that will allow you to leverage your existing network in order to create opportunities for new networking in the short, medium and long term.

Identify where you will build your network

Your evaluation of your network will probably throw up a lot of useful information for this action. You need to decide where will you need to go to network with potential contacts and where can you refresh relationships with people you have fallen out of touch with. You have so many choices about where to build your network, it is important to make some decisions and begin to test them out. Procrastination is the enemy of networking.

Make decisions, start networking and then amend and refine your approach based on your results. If you find you have made the wrong decisions, then simply try again by changing where you are networking. Here are some of the quick decisions you can make:

- Which membership association(s) you could usefully join and participate in.
- Which online platform it be most fruitful to be part of (because you haven't chosen the option to opt out of the online world, have you?).
- The geographical area(s) you are going to focus on.
- Your target organisations.
- What kind of professional and job level you need connect with (influencers or decision-makers).

Again, the key here is to make some decisions, take some actions, test out your decisions and then appraise whether you want to change them or if you got it right. If you think about it for too long you will just miss out on opportunities which other people will be benefitting from instead of you.

Renew contact with three dormant contacts

This is a real quick win, it sounds super easy but takes a bit of bravery to do. In everyone's network there are people they wish they had not fallen out of contact with, and you are unlikely to be an exception. You are likely to have colleagues from previous work, former customers and clients, or friends from school or college you can usefully reconnect with.

Life and work get busy and it is easy to run out of the time to keep up with everyone. This is inevitable, but dangerous for the health of your network. Every so often it is worth reviewing if you need to reconnect with specific people. It is very easy to convince yourself that these people will have no interest in speaking to you any more. Your inner voice may say *Well they haven't contacted you so what makes you think they want to speak to you,* or, *They have contacted you so why put the time into them?* But resist that downward thought spiral, and pick up the phone.

In reality people often welcome a call from an old contact or friend, the opportunity to say hello again, to catch up and to share what has been happening. So a simple email or call to say *I was wondering how you were. How's life going?* can be all it takes to revive the contact. Offer a coffee, cup of tea, lunch or just a chat, find out what you still have in common, then begin to build the relationship forward from there. It can help to start with the easier contacts (those you feel the closest affinity with, and most regret your lack of contact with). Then begin to work towards the contacts you have left for a longer period, or you see as being primarily business-related and with fewer clear common interests. Alternatively you could go with the jump in and get wet philosophy by contacting the difficult ones first. You know yourself best and therefore know which way round is likely to lead to success.

Prepare some networking introductions

These are an important part of your preparation for networking. A variety of succinct, interesting and memorable introductions are vital tools in your networking tool kit (how you make your impact). Working out what you want to say beforehand improves your confidence, leaving you free to focus on the other person and their response, rather than being distracted by working out what to say on the spur of the moment.

Your introduction should vary based on the context you are in, the type of networking you are doing, the location, the theme of the event and so on. Having a range of introductions ready to suit a variety of scenarios leaves you free to focus on other event preparation.

After your networking, review what worked well, which introductions produced the best discussion or level of interest, and reflect on why you think that was. Use the experience to improve your introductions and maximise their conversation-opening effectiveness.

Add three new contacts to your internal network

Your internal network needs to be looked after as much as your external network, so cultivate it. Who are the people currently supporting you, providing the expertise you need to provide to your clients, or supporting you in the delivery of what you do? Evaluate your internal network with as much attention as you did your external network, and identify areas of weakness so that you can begin to address them quickly.

These questions may help you:
- What subjects make me feel uncomfortable when a client asks questions?
- What are the latest big challenges in my industry, and who knows about them?
- What are our competitors' USPs and who can help us emulate them?
- Who have I worked with and not really known what they do or how they do it?

The answers will identify the areas where you need to improve your internal network and the people you need to reach. The beauty of internal networking is that it is almost always a mutual activity: the people you are contacting need to network with you too, so it is win, win for everyone.

Another quick action in this category is to make sure you have stayed in contact with everyone you have worked with recently. If you have been part of an engagement, contract or project, then have you ensured the people involved are a continuing part of your network? If not, follow up with them, share and reconfirm knowledge gained in the course of the contract. Explore if and how you could help each other in the future. You may be able to make referrals for each other as a result of taking the time to do this.

Expand your general and specialist knowledge

We all need sources of material for conversation, and luckily for us there are many different ways of obtaining it. If you are a professional you should regularly read appropriate broadsheet articles (online or in print), serious non-fiction, and articles in high-level magazines and journals. There is a wealth of sources of further information: professional bodies, TED, the BBC, specialist podcasts and so on. One of the useful features of social media is that our friends act as curators and suppliers of the kind of information that interests us. By deciding how to keep abreast of what is around us, we can ensure we are never stuck for informative and interesting conversation.

Follow up with someone you met recently

For me the single greatest waste of all networking energy and effort is the failure to follow up. Almost everyone is guilty of this at some time or other, so it really pays dividends to get into good follow-up habits. All the physical and emotional effort you have made will be wasted if you fail to follow up with people.

Look back at the networking you have done recently. Is there anyone you have met who you haven't followed up with yet? If so, do it now.

One of the inescapable truths of networking is the longer you leave follow-ups, the harder they become, so the key is to take simple follow-on steps quickly. An email or call to say "Hello, it was great to meet you," will be a helpful start. Some people do these from the train home, or immediately after a meeting. The sooner the better, and this is one area in which you do not run the risk of looking too keen. If you refer to the conversations you had, or even better include a new piece of relevant information (often via a hyperlink), you have been immediately helpful.

Now it really is up to you

If you don't put time into your network then don't be surprised when it doesn't put time into you. A little investment maintained over a long period builds a network of people to support, develop, promote and celebrate with you.

Take what works for you from this book, adapt and improve upon it. It is time for you to take some actions. They do not need to be big or ground-breaking. They just need to happen.

ABOUT THE AUTHOR

For two decades, Adrian Priddle has been training business executives from top management consultancies, accountancy practices and legal firms to overcome the awkwardness and fear of professional networking.

Using the *GLAD Networking* approach developed out of his extensive experience, Adrian has enabled thousands of professionals to develop an approach to networking that enables their qualities and personalities to shine, and their businesses to prosper.

Lightning Source UK Ltd.
Milton Keynes UK
UKOW03f1301230417
299676UK00002B/27/P